THE PREPARATION
OF ARCHAEOLOGICAL REPORTS

The Preparation
of Archaeological Reports

LESLIE GRINSELL
PHILIP RAHTZ
DAVID PRICE WILLIAMS

St. Martin's Press
New York

Duplicated editions of this work were issued in
1962 (250 copies) and 1963 (350 copies) by the
Bristol Archaeological Research Group from
Bristol City Museum.
First (printed) edition 1966
Second (printed) edition 1974

© 1974 Leslie Grinsell, Philip Rahtz and David Price Williams

All rights reserved. For information, write:
St. Martin's Press, Inc., 175 Fifth Avenue, New York, N.Y. 10010
Printed in Great Britain
Library of Congress Catalog Card Number: 74–82135
First published in the United States of America in 1974

AFFILIATED PUBLISHERS: Macmillan Limited, London
—also at Bombay, Calcutta, Madras and Melbourne

CONTENTS

LIST OF ILLUSTRATIONS

PREFACE TO THE SECOND (PRINTED) EDITION

In most regions, not only in the United Kingdom but also elsewhere, the zest for archaeological digging is so often greater than the desire or the ability to prepare for publication a written report on the work done and the results achieved.

The original duplicated editions of this work (1962 and 1963), issued by the Bristol Archaeological Research Group as its first publication, were directed towards solving this problem in its own region. For the first printed edition (1966) the scope was widened to cover the rest of the British Isles. As this work is now used in universities and libraries in the U.S.A. and is consulted also by students of classical archaeology, the scope of the present edition has been slightly extended to meet at least some of the needs of this wider range of coming archaeologists.

The authors are aware that some of the procedures here recommended are not universally agreed. The book will serve its purpose if it forms a basis for discussion among lecturers, students and others. It is *not* intended that all archaeological reports should be forced into this particular straitjacket. It *is* intended as a Guide which will enable the potential writer of archaeological reports to infuse into them his own individuality or even originality, within the framework of what is required by editors and publishers.

The first duplicated edition of this work was not quite the first book on the subject to be published. This seems to have been *Jak Publikować Źródła Archeologiczne* (*The Publication of Archaeological Sources*), By Włodzimierz Hołubowicz, published in Warsaw in 1961. There is a copy in the University of London Institute of Archaeology, 31/34 Gordon Square, London WC1H 0PY, and it contains fairly full summaries in French and Russian.

ACKNOWLEDGMENTS

The authors are grateful to the undermentioned organizations or persons for assistance received:

The Council for British Archaeology, for kindly allowing the use of their list of abbreviations for titles of archaeological periodicals.

The Prehistoric Society and Dr John Coles, for permitting reproduction of Fig. 13.

Adams & Dart Ltd., Frances Lynch, and Colin Burgess, publishers and editors of *Prehistoric Man in Wales and the West*, for permission to reproduce parts of an essay by one of the authors (L.V.G.) in Chapter 6.

The Institute of Archaeology, London University, and Mrs S. C. Humphreys for permission to use some material from a Research Seminar held at their premises in 1967, on the publication of archaeological reports.

Miss Beatrice de Cardi, O.B.E., late Assistant Secretary of the Council for British Archaeology, for information and advice on C.B.A. publication grants.

Miss Cherry Lavell, Editor of C.B.A. Abstracts, for help in drafting the section on Abstracts.

Dr. Isobel F. Smith, Editor, *Wiltshire Archaeol. Natur. Hist. Mag.*, for several suggestions.

Mr. Alan Warhurst, B.A., F.S.A., F.M.A., whose text in Chapter 2 of the first (printed) edition has formed the basis for the present Chapter 3.

Mrs. Frances Neale, B.A., for several useful suggestions made at galley proof stage.

Mr. D. G. Buckley for permission to reproduce the location map from 'The Excavation of Two Slate Cairns at Trevone, Padstow, 1972', *Cornish Archaeology*, No. 11.

Mr. Peter Bellwood for permission to reproduce the site plan from 'Fortifications and Economy in Prehistoric New Zealand', *Proc. Prehist. Soc.*, Vol. XXXVII.

Professor Stuart Piggott for permission to reproduce the trench plan from 'Excavations of a Stone Circle at Croft Moraig, Perthshire, Scotland', *Proc. Prehist. Soc.*, Vol. XXXVII.

Miss Sheila Gibson and Tim Tatton-Brown for permission to reproduce Figures 5 and 6, and also Professor Iris Love.

ABBREVIATIONS FOR TITLES OF PERIODICALS ON ARCHAEOLOGY AND RELATED SUBJECTS

Introductory note

The following list is, with the exception of a very few items marked with an asterisk (*), that recommended by the Council for British Archaeology. Their present list is an edition of their list first published in 1968, to which later periodicals have been added and from which those now defunct have been removed. One of the authors (L.V.G.) has always considered many of these abbreviations to be too long, and that they should be treated as a guide rather than always slavishly followed. The rapidly increasing cost of printing may lead to the adoption of shorter forms of abbreviation, such as *P.* for *Proc.*, and *T.* for *Trans.* Most of the general and national societies and periodicals have their own systems of shorter abbreviation with which the majority of their readers are already familiar. In the opinion of the author (L.V.G.) there is no reason why any county or regional society should not shorten the abbreviation for its own publication to the form which it has always used, e.g. *B.A.J.* for *Berkshire Archaeol. J.*

A study of this list, which includes only the current periodicals, should enable any author of a report to devise his own abbreviation on similar lines for older periodicals now defunct, e.g. *The Antiquary*, *The Reliquary*, the *Archaeological News Letter*, and many others which contain a great deal of useful material liable to get overlooked.

The great advantage of abbreviations in these extended forms is that being self-explanatory they need no key; but that would apply even if a little careful pruning were done.

International, national, and general periodicals

Advan. Sci.
Agr. Hist. Rev.
**Amer. J. Archaeol.*
Antiq. J.
Antiquity
Apollo
Archaeologia
Archaeol. Bibliogr.
Archaeol. J.
Archaeol. Rev. (C.B.A. Groups 12 & 13)
Archaeometry

Britannia
Brit. Archaeol. Abstr.
Brit. Mus. Quart.
Brit. Numis. J.
Bull. Hist. Metall. Group
Bull. Inst. Hist. Res.
Burlington Mag.

Chem. Brit.
**Coin Medal Bull.* (Seaby)
Connoisseur
Counc. Brit. Archaeol. Rep.
Curr. Archaeol.

Econ. Hist. Rev.
Endeavour
Engl. Hist. Rev.

Fld. Stud.
Folk Life
Folklore

Geogr. J.
Geol. Mag.

Hist. J.
History
Hist. Today

Illus. London News
Int. J. Naut. Archaeol.

J. Arms Armour Soc.
J. Brit. Archaeol. Ass.
J. Brit. Ceram. Soc.
J. Brit. Soc. Master Glasspainters
J. Engl. Place Name Soc.
J. Roman Stud.
J. Soil Sci.
J. Warburg Courtauld Inst.

Local Hist.

Man
**Mariner's Mirror*
Medieval Archaeol.
Mercian Geol.

*Midland Hist.
Museums J.

Nat. Monuments Rec. Rep.
Nature (London)
New Phytol.
New Sci.
Northern Hist.
Numis. Chron.
*Numis. Circ.

Phil. Trans. Roy. Soc. London
Post-Medieval Archaeol.
Proc. Brit. Acad.
Proc. Brit. Ceram. Soc.
Proc. Geol. Ass.
Proc. Prehist. Soc.
Proc. Roy. Anthropol. Inst. Gr. Brit. Ir.
Proc. Roy. Inst. Gr. Brit.
Proc. Roy. Soc. London

Sagabook (of the Viking Soc. for Northern Research)
Sci. (&) Archaeol.
Sci. J.
S.E. Natur. Antiq.
Stud. Conserv.
Stud. Speleol. (J. Ass. Pengelly Cave Res. Centre)

Trans. Ancient Monuments Soc.
Trans. Inst. Brit. Geogr.
Trans. Monumental Brass Soc.

Vernacular Architect.
Victoria Albert Mus. Ybk.

World Archaeol.

County and regional publications in the British Isles

ENGLAND

Bedfordshire	Bedfordshire Archaeol. J.
	Bedfordshire Mag.
Berkshire	Berkshire Archaeol. J.
	Trans. Newbury Dist. Fld. Club
Buckinghamshire	Rec. Buckinghamshire
	Wolverton Hist. J., now: Milton Keynes J. Archaeol. Hist.

Cambridgeshire	*Proc. Cambridge Antiq. Soc.*
	Cambridge Hist. J.
Cheshire	*J. Chester Archaeol. Soc.*
	Trans. Hist. Soc. Lancashire Cheshire
	Trans. Lancashire Cheshire Antiq. Soc.
Cornwall	*J. Roy. Inst. Cornwall*
	Cornish Archaeol.
	Devon Cornwall Notes Queries
Cumberland	*Trans. Cumberland Westmorland Antiq. Archaeol. Soc.*
Derbyshire	*Derbyshire Archaeol. J.*
Devon	*Proc. Devon Archaeol. Soc.*
	Trans. Devonshire Ass.
	Devon Hist.
	Devon Cornwall Notes Queries
	Trans. Proc. Torquay Natur. Hist. Soc.
Dorset	*Proc. Dorset Natur. Hist. Archaeol. Soc.*
	Notes Queries Somerset Dorset
Durham	*Durham Univ. J.*
	Trans. Architect. Archaeol. Soc. Durham Northumberland
	Pap. S. Shields Archaeol. Hist. Soc.
	Antiq. Sunderland
Essex	*Trans. Essex Archaeol. Soc.*
	Essex Natur.
Gloucestershire	*Trans. Bristol Gloucestershire Archaeol. Soc.*
	Proc. Cotteswold Natur. Fld. Club
	Proc. Univ. Bristol Spelæol. Soc.
Hampshire	*Proc. Hampshire Fld. Club Archaeol. Soc.*
	Proc. Isle Wight Natur. Hist. Archaeol. Soc.
Herefordshire	*Trans. Woolhope Natur. Fld. Club*
Hertfordshire	*Hertfordshire Archaeol.*
	Hertfordshire Past Present
	Rickmansworth Hist.
Huntingdonshire	*Rec. Huntingdonshire*
Kent	*Archaeol. Cantiana* (Kent Archaeological Society)
	Faversham Mag.
	Kent Archaeol. Rev.
	Proc. Crayford Manor House Hist. Archaeol. Soc.
Lancashire	*Trans. Hist. Soc. Lancashire Cheshire*
	Trans. Lancashire Cheshire Antiq. Soc.
Leicestershire	*Trans. Leicestershire Archaeol. Hist. Soc.*
Lincolnshire	*Lincolnshire Hist. Archaeol.*
London	*Guildhall Misc.*
	J. London Soc.

	London Archaeol.
	London Natur.
	Trans. London Middlesex Archaeol. Soc.
	Univ. London Inst. Archaeol. Bull.
Norfolk	*Norfolk Archaeol.*
Northamptonshire	*J. Northampton Mus. Art Gallery*
	Northamptonshire Past Present
	J. Northamptonshire Natur. Hist. Soc. Fld. Club
	Rep. Pap. Northamptonshire Antiq. Soc.
Northumberland	*Archaeol. Aeliana* (Publication of the Society of Antiquaries of Newcastle-upon-Tyne)
	Trans. Architect. Archaeol. Soc. Durham Northumberland
Nottinghamshire	*Trans. Thoroton Soc. Nottinghamshire*
	Thoroton Soc. Rec. Ser.
	Nottingham Medieval Stud.
Oxfordshire	*Oxoniensia* (Oxford Architect. Hist. Soc.)
	Oxfordshire Rec. Soc.
Shropshire	*Trans. Shropshire Archaeol. Soc.*
Somerset	*Somerset Archaeol. Natur. Hist.*
	Notes Queries Somerset Dorset
	Proc. Univ. Bristol Spelæol. Soc.
Staffordshire	*N. Staffordshire J. Fld. Stud.*
	Trans. S. Staffordshire Archaeol. Hist. Soc. (formerly Lichfield S. Staffordshire . . .)
Suffolk	*Proc. Suffolk Inst. Archaeol.*
Surrey	*Surrey Archaeol. Collect.*
	Proc. Croydon Natur. Hist. Sci. Soc.
	Proc. Leatherhead Dist. Local Hist. Soc.
Sussex	*Sussex Archaeol. Collect.*
Warwickshire	*Trans. Birmingham Warwickshire Archaeol. Soc.*
	Proc. Coventry Dist. Natur. Hist. Sci. Soc.
Westmorland	*Trans. Cumberland Westmorland Antiq. Archaeol. Soc.*
Wiltshire	*Wiltshire Archaeol. Natur. Hist. Mag.*
Worcestershire	*Trans. Worcestershire Archaeol. Soc.*
	Vale Evesham Hist. Soc. Res. Pap.
Yorkshire	*Yorkshire Archaeol. J.*
	Annu. Rep. Yorkshire Phil. Soc.
	Bradford Antiq.
	E. Riding Archaeol.
	Publ. Thoresby Soc.
	Ryedale Hist.
	Trans. Halifax Antiq. Soc.
	Trans. Hunter Archaeol. Soc.

CHANNEL ISLANDS
Bull. Annu. Soc. Jersiaise
Quart. Rev. Guernsey Soc.
Rep. Trans. Soc. Guernesiaise

ISLE OF MAN
Proc. Isle Man Natur. Hist. Antiq. Soc.
J. Manx Mus.

NORTHERN IRELAND
Ulster J. Archaeol.

IRISH REPUBLIC
General
J. Roy. Soc. Antiq. Ir.
Ir. Hist. Stud.
Ir. Speleol.
Ir. Sword
Proc. Royal Ir. Acad.

Counties
Cork	*J. Cork Hist. Archaeol. Soc.*
Galway	*J. Galway Archaeol. Hist. Soc.*
Kerry	*J. Kerry Archaeol. Hist. Soc.*
Kildare	*J. County Kildare Archaeol. Soc.*
Louth	*County Louth Archaeol. J.*
Meath	*Riocht na Midhe* (Rec. Meath Archaeol. Hist. Soc.)
Munster	*N. Munster Antiq. J.*
Wexford	*J. Old Wexford Soc.*

SCOTLAND
General
Discovery Excavation Scot. (C.B.A. Group I)
Proc. Soc. Antiq. Scot.
Scot. Archaeol. Forum
Scot. Art Rev.
Scot. Geogr. Mag.
Scot. Hist. Rev.
Scot. Stud.

Counties
Ayrshire	*Ayrshire Archaeol. Natur. Hist. Soc. Collect.*
Berwickshire	*Hist. Berwickshire Natur. Club*
Buteshire	*Trans. Buteshire Natur. Hist. Soc.*
Dumfriesshire }	*Trans. Dumfriesshire Galloway Natur. Hist.*
Kirkcudbright }	*Antiq. Soc.*
Lanarkshire	*Glasgow Archaeol. J.*
Lothian (East)	*Trans. E. Lothian Antiq. Fld. Natur. Soc.*
Perthshire	*Trans. Proc. Perthshire Soc. Natur. Sci.*
Roxburghshire	*Trans. Hawick Archaeol. Soc.*

WALES

General	*Archaeol. Cambrensis* (Cambrian Archaeol. Ass.)
	Bull. Board Celtic Stud.
	J. Hist. Soc. Church Wales
	Welsh Hist. Rev.
County Societies	
Anglesey	*Trans. Anglesey Antiq. Soc. Fld. Club*
Breconshire	*Brycheiniog*
Caernarvonshire	*Trans. Caernarvonshire Hist. Soc.*
Cardiganshire	*Ceredigion*
Carmarthen	*Carmarthen Antiq.*
Denbighshire	*Trans. Denbighshire Hist. Soc.*
Flintshire	*Flintshire Hist. Soc. Publ.*
Glamorganshire	*Glamorgan Hist.*
	Morgannwg (Trans. Glamorgan Local Hist. Soc.)
	Trans. Cardiff Natur. Soc.
Merioneth	*J. Merioneth Hist. Rec. Soc.*
Monmouthshire	*Monmouthshire Antiq.*
Montgomeryshire	*Montgomeryshire Collect.*
Radnorshire	*Trans. Radnorshire Soc.*

Periodicals mainly on foreign archaeology

The following list is based on that issued by the *American Journal of Archaeology*. An asterisk in the column headed BSA indicates that the same form of abbreviation is used by the British School at Athens; where they use a different form it is stated. The list includes some British periodicals dealing mainly with foreign archaeology. It will be noted that the policy followed by both these publishing bodies, and of most others in foreign archaeology, is to abbreviate more drastically than is recommended for British periodicals by the Council for British Archaeology. To some extent this different policy results from the largely international character of most of these periodicals and of Egyptian, Greek and Roman archaeology, attracting a higher percentage of professional scholars. It is not the practice to abbreviate titles comprising one word only, e.g. *Berytus*. There is an obvious need for an internationally agreed system of abbreviations for the titles of all well established archaeological periodicals. Publications dealing almost entirely with philology are excluded, as are most of those in languages other than English, French, Italian, and German. Only a selection of the last three is included. Items added by the authors are preceded by a dagger (†).

		BSA
AA	*Archäologischer Anzeiger*	*
AAA	*Athens Annals of Archaeology*	
ActaA	*Acta Archaeologica*	*ActArch*
AJA	*American Journal of Archaeology*	*

		BSA
AnatSt	*Anatolian Studies*	
AnnLiv	*Annals of Archaeology & Anthropology, Liverpool*	*LAAA*
AntDenk	*Antike Denkmäler*	*AD*
ArchEph	*Archaiologike Ephemeris*	*AE*
ASAE	*Annales du Service des antiquités de l'Égypte*	
AssyrS	*Assyriological Studies*	
AthMitt	*Mitteilungen des deutschen archäologischen Instituts, Athenische Abteilung*	*AM*
AZ	*Archäologische Zeitung*	*
BASOR	*Bulletin of American Schools of Oriental Research*	
BASPR	*Bulletin of American School of Prehistoric Research*	
BCH	*Bulletin de Correspondence Hellénique*	*
BIFAO	*Bulletin de l'Institut français d'archéologie Orientale*	
BJPES	*Bulletin of Jewish Palestine Exploration Society*	
BMFA	*Bulletin of Museum of Fine Arts, Boston, U.S.A.*	
BMMA	*Bulletin of Metropolitan Museum of Art, New York*	*BullMetrMus*
BMQ	*British Museum Quarterly*	*
BonnJbb	*Bonner Jahrbücher*	*BJ*
BPI	*Bolletino di Paletnologia Italiana*	*
BSA	*Annual of British School at Athens*	*
BSPF	*Bulletin de la Société Préhistorique française*	
BSR	*British School at Rome, Papers*	*
Cd'E	*Chronique d'Égypte*	
CIE	*Corpus Inscriptionum Etruscarum*	
CIG	*Corpus Inscriptionum Graecarum*	*
CIL	*Corpus Instriptionum Latinarum*	*
CQ	*Classical Quarterly*	*
CR	*Classical Review*	*
DOPapers	*Dumbarton Oaks Papers*	
FA	*Fasti Archaeologici*	
GGA	*Göttingische Gelehrte Anzeigen*	*
HSCP	*Harvard Studies in Classical Philology*	*HarvSt*
†*IEJ*	*Israel Exploration Journal*	
IG	*Inscriptiones Graecae*	*
IGR	*Inscriptiones Graecae ad Res Romanas pertinentes*	*
JAOS	*Journal of American Oriental Society*	
JdI	*Jahrbuch des k. deutschen archäologischen Instituts*	*
JEA	*Journal of Egyptian Archaeology*	*
JHS	*Journal of Hellenic Studies*	*

BSA

JNES	*Journal of Near Eastern Studies*	
JPOS	*Journal of Palestine Oriental Society*	
JRAI	*Journal of Royal Anthropological Institute*	*
JRS	*Journal of Roman Studies*	*
JWarb	*Journal of Warburg & Courtauld Institute*	
†*Levant*	*Levant,* Journal of British School of Archaeology in Jerusalem	
MAAR	*Memoirs of American Academy at Rome*	*MemAmAc*
MAMA	*Monumenta Asiae Minoris Antiqua*	*
MonAnt	*Monumenti Antichi . . . dei Lincei*	*MA*
MonInst	*Monumenti dell' Instituto*	*
MonPiot	*Monuments . . . Piot*	*
NC	*Numismatic Chronicle*	*NumChron*
NSc	*Notizie degli Scavi di Antichità*	*NS*
OpusArch	*Opuscula Archaeologica*	*OpArch*
PAAR	*Papers & Monographs of American Academy in Rome*	
PEFA	*Palestine Exploration Fund Annual*	
PEQ	*Palestine Exploration Quarterly*	*
ProcBritAc	*Proceedings of British Academy*	
ProcJPES	*Proceedings of Jewish Palestine Exploration Society*	
ProcPS	*Proceedings of Prehistoric Society*	
PZ	*Prähistorische Zeitschrift*	*
QDAP	*Quarterly of Department of Antiquities of Palestine*	*
RA	*Revue archéologique*	*
REA	*Revue des Études Anciennes*	*
RecTrav	*Recueil de travaux . . . égyptiennes et assyriennes*	
REG	*Revue des Études Grecques*	*
RendLinc	*Rendiconti della R. Accademia dei Lincei*	*
RevÉgyptol.	*Revue égyptologique.* Paris	
RomMitt	*Mitteilungen des deutschen archäologische Instituts, Römische Abteilung*	*RM*
StEtr	*Studi Etruschi*	*SE*
SymbOslo	*Symbolae Osloenses*	
TAPA	*Transactions & Proceedings of American Philological Association*	*
UPMB	*University of Pennsylvania Museum Bulletin*	
WPZ	*Wiener prähistorische Zeitschrift*	
YWCS	*Year's Work in Classical Studies*	

I

THE FORM OF PUBLICATION

Philip Rahtz

> Gracious my lord
> I should report that which I say I saw
> But know not how to do it.
> *Macbeth*, act V, scene iv

At the time when the first (printed) edition of this book was published in 1966, it was widely held that archaeologists should publish their work fully, in as much detail as possible, in a permanent form, available to anyone who wanted to read it in a good library. The following chapters are still based on this assumption; but in the years that have passed since the first edition, all the problems of full publication that were hinted at then have become more acute. A crisis is imminent, if indeed it does not already exist, because of rapidly rising printing costs. It seems fitting then to begin this book with a discussion on why archaeologists do publish their work, whether they need to do so fully, what are the alternatives to the printed page bound between covers, and whether the advice contained in this book will remain relevant for more than the next two or three decades.

The problem

It is a generally (but not universally) accepted fact that archaeologists should publish the evidence on which they base historical conclusions. The minority of dissentients, which includes some editors and others, suggests that details of the evidence should be deposited with the finds and only 'interpretative' summary reports should be published; and that moreover there is no such thing as 'objective' evidence: the data recovered from excavations are as subjective as the conclusions drawn from them.

Until recent years there have been no great difficulties in publishing the evidence: the amount that was recovered was relatively slight and, in any case, overshadowed by 'interesting' speculative material and discussion. A notable exception was the work of Pitt-Rivers, in which the detailed evidence vastly outweighed the section on discussion. It was possible for Pitt-Rivers and certain other early writers to publish without regard for cost because they had private resources, and because printing was relatively cheap.

Difficulties have arisen because (a) more detail is now being recorded on the site; (b) specialist reports on site and material have become longer and more numerous; (c) more excavation is being done without a corresponding increase in the media available for publication; (d) archaeological reports are becoming more unreadable to the layman; (e) printing costs have increased substantially and are likely to continue to rise.

Many editors of national, regional and county periodical publications are becoming increasingly unwilling to accept reports with detail that is seldom read or understood by their members or subscribers. Others, one feels, accept detailed material only because they feel that they ought to.

The largely amateur background to British archaeology seems to militate against the publication of archaeological and scientific work in the large well-produced formats characteristic of the state-aided and professionally backed German, Dutch and Scandinavian bodies. The Directorate of Ancient Monuments in this country make subventions to national and regional bodies for periodicals and monographs and arrange publication of H.M.S.O. monographs. These last are produced with delays which have on occasions been up to ten years from submission of the typescript to publication of the monograph. Paradoxically the more important the site, the less detail can be published because of length and expense; a single trench can be adequately published while extensive excavations of sites covering several hectares are increasingly difficult to place. It has, however, now become difficult not merely to publish detail, but to publish at all. Queues are building up of one, two or more years' delay in many media. This is *before* the anticipated expansion of rescue archaeology has really got fully under way.

The situation may now be summarized. There are three grades of archaeological reportage as seen from the editor's or reader's point of view: (a) the conclusions, hypotheses, syntheses and interesting finds; (b) the exposition of the evidence; (c) the detail of the stratification, features, finds and scientific reports on which (a) and (b) are based. Only (a) is really editorially acceptable; (b) is mostly unread but recognized as necessary; (c) is unpalatable, and wanted only by those seriously involved in the subject.

These problems are common to rescue and research projects of excavation and fieldwork. It is a paradox that the difficulties of publication apply more to the *evidence* which is unique and unrepeatable, than to the *interpretation* and *discussion* which could be done at anytime.

Possible solutions

In general there are four solutions to these problems:

(a) To keep on fighting for full and detailed publication in hard print, on the model of that achieved by our continental colleagues and those further afield in, e.g. Australia; to press for more Government subsidies in the same way that we have successfully fought for more money for rescue excavation; to increase the media for publishing the increased output by creating new regional, national, period, and subject periodicals.

(b) As (a), but to seek to reduce costs by:

    i. the use of offset litho and other cheaper methods, with less use of half-tone;

    ii. cutting out commercial printing costs by private publications, such as Brodribb and others (1968 onwards) and Branigan (1971), with greater use of do-it-yourself techniques such as those used in producing Brodribb and others (1968 onwards); the difference is between the £1–£2 of these publications and the £10–£12 now being reached by commercial and even University presses;

    iii. seek wider circulation to reduce unit costs.

(c) To be selective in what is published in whatever form, relegating the rest to archive status as detailed below.

(d) To institute some form of nationally agreed massive shorthand and abbreviation scheme such as that recently suggested in Smith (1970) for the description of pottery.

If it is thought desirable to relegate *evidence* to archives, who will decide what to exclude? It may be the author, who only submits a truncated or subjective script containing the cream of his material; or it may be the editor, who deletes material only after he is satisfied that it does in fact support the conclusions reached, i.e. he will insist on a full and complete text *as if it were to be fully published*, subsequently deleting those parts which he considers suitable for archive form only. The best solution is probably that it should be decided by mutual agreement, the author indicating what he believes should be in permanent form.

It is doubtful whether any nationally agreed guidelines can be laid down as to what is worthy of full and permanent record. What is *record*? It may be valid to publish *record* which is of permanent value, rather than *comment* which is evanescent. Comment, interpretation, or synthesis are repeatable experiments which vary with whatever archaeological model happens to be fashionable at the time.

If it is agreed that material is to be deleted, it must be decided what is going to happen to it. It could be published as a separate expensive volume to be acquired only by libraries, institutions and wealthy people. Alternatively it might be published as a separate, cheaply produced and bound supplement to the rest. This may be printed in some way or made available in xerox copies, on microfilm or computer tapes. Whatever its fate it must be indexed by references in the published version, to inform the reader how it can be obtained or consulted, e.g. in the National Monuments Record, or the Archaeology Division of the Ordnance

Survey Office at Southampton, or in the Library of the Society of Antiquaries of London. Emphasis must in any case be on availability and integration of reference into published text.

One feature of British archaeology is the proliferation of regional news sheets. Some concern has been expressed that they sometimes include material which is never published elsewhere. They are undoubtedly suitable for quick dissemination of interim reports, and as a platform for comment of a transient kind, unsuited to the immortality of the hard archive, published or not. If material does find its way into them which never sees final permanent publication, it may be regrettable, but preferable to its never being recorded anywhere.

The next generation may see the end of the printed, bound journal with which we are familiar today. It may prove to be more economical to subscribe to a national service which will issue photolithograph copies of papers related to the subjects or periods selected by the subscriber, rather like a press-cutting service, or selected from a regularly issued index of papers. In this there would be no editing involved. Authors would send a full and perfect manuscript or typescript to the producer, who would immediately make it available to subscribers, perhaps within a matter of weeks. The cost of such a subscription, even to a commercially run service, might be no higher than the £20–£50 per annum which most professional archaeologists now subscribe to bound journals or to societies issuing them.

A series of monographs called *British Archaeological Reports* (122 Banbury Road, Oxford OX2 7BP) has recently been launched. Its five-page *Notes for Contributors* contains numerous useful points. Authors are required to submit their papers typed on an electric typewriter with a carbon ribbon, and to leave adequate margins on all four sides of each sheet, which has to be international A4 size and of good quality. Advice on headings, sub-headings, and tabulation is particularly useful. Each page has to be submitted free from blemish of any kind.

Another possibility is that the written report will be replaced by an audio-visual report, or a combination of the two. For some time archaeologists have been aware that the best way of explaining to other people what the results of an excavation have been is by a spoken exposition of a series of colour slides, as in a teaching lecture. The best record of what an excavation looked like is a set of colour slides, few or none of which ever get published. The few black and white photographs which do get into the final report are a poor substitute for the numerous colour pictures which are now commonly taken of every excavation.

Will the future report be a set of colour slides with a sound tape which takes the reader step by step through the whole excavation and its interpretation? Or might it be a videotape which combines both? A compromise would be a set of slides or a filmstrip supplied with a written commentary. A recent example of this was the set of slides on *Rescue Archaeology* issued by RESCUE[1] with a lengthy duplicated

---

[1] RESCUE, a Trust for British Archaeology, 25A The Tything, Worcester. Sets of this and other material are obtainable from this organisation.

commentary. Several hundred of these sets were sold and ensured the widespread dissemination of information to hundreds of audiences who could not have been reached by the written word.

These are matters for the future. Meanwhile, whatever method of publication is eventually decided, it is still the responsibility of every archaeologist to produce a full and detailed record of the work undertaken, illustrated by adequate line and half-tone illustrations, with references to the location and availability of 'archive' material including not only the finds and field records but also colour slides and photographs, and monochrome photographs.

What happens to this report is a matter for subsequent negotiation, but the full report is the essential basis from which any other kind of report will be developed. It is to the archaeologist about to produce the full report that the following chapters are addressed.

2

PRELIMINARIES AND INITIAL STAGES

Leslie Grinsell

> A discovery dates only from the time of the record of it,
> and not from the time of its being found in the soil.
> PITT-RIVERS, *Excavations in Cranborne Chase*, iv (1898), 28

Publication grants

In view of the increasing costs of publication, it is well to begin this chapter with a brief statement regarding the sources from which it is possible to obtain grants towards the publication of archaeological material. The Council for British Archaeology (8 St. Andrew's Place, Regent's Park, London NW1 4LB) provides at present (1973) a total of £2,000 per annum in publication grants, the awards being made once a year. Editors who intend submitting papers should do so by 18 March each year, and the awards are generally announced during June. The grants are made specifically for papers of either national or regional importance and cover all periods from prehistoric to industrial archaeology in the British Isles. To be eligible the submitting Society must be affiliated to the C.B.A. and not in receipt of State funds. Grants are not awarded for publication of interim reports. Occasionally the C.B.A. Advisory Panel awards a grant on condition that certain improvements are made in either the text or the illustrations of the paper submitted. Therefore it is preferable not to go to press until the award has been announced. Editors intending to submit papers should note that if a report is accompanied by large drawings, the latter should be submitted in the form of photographic or other copies, reduced to the scale at which it is intended to reproduce them.

The Colt Fund Awards, made annually, include the cost of preparing drawings for archaeological publication. Further details are obtainable from the Secretary, Society for Medieval Archaeology, University College, Gower Street, London WC1E 6BT. Applications should be submitted by mid-February.

The Directorate of Ancient Monuments, Department of the Environment

(Fortress House, 23 Savile Row, London W1X 1AB) normally gives grants towards the cost of publishing reports on excavations undertaken under its auspices. The British Academy (Burlington House, Piccadilly, London W1V 0HS) sometimes gives grants towards archaeological publications.

It should be noted that responsibility for submitting papers for grants rests with the editors of the appropriate periodicals, and *not* with the authors of the papers.

Choice of publications

It is desirable to discuss publication with the editor of an archaeological periodical before the paper has been started. The size of the page and block size will then be known, and also the general style and conventions to which the paper is expected to conform. A major difficulty of actually booking space beforehand arises if the paper is to include specialist reports, since the author of the main paper is usually in a position to estimate neither the length of the specialist reports, nor when they are likely to be ready. The choice is between publications which can be classified as under:

(a) INTERNATIONAL PERIODICALS such as *Current Anthropology*, *World Archaeology*, *Proc. Prehist. Soc.* (though largely British), and the *Internat. J. Naut. Archaeol.* Papers published in the first three are normally written by mature archaeologists who have fresh material of fundamental importance and wide appeal to communicate.

(b) NATIONAL PERIODICALS, for reports covering more than one county; reports on matters of more than local interest; or for summaries of more detailed reports to be published elsewhere. In this category are the *Proceedings of the Prehistoric Society*; the *Journal of Roman Studies* and *Britannia* (the British section of the last); *Medieval Archaeology*; the *Journal of Post Medieval Archaeology*; and the *Journal of Industrial Archaeology*. The publications just mentioned are suitable only for papers the subject matter of which is limited to one or other of those periods. For papers covering more than one period the following periodicals are available: the *Antiquaries Journal*; *Archaeologia*; the *Archaeological Journal*; and the *Journal of the British Archaeological Association*.

(c) REGIONAL OR LOCAL PERIODICALS, for papers dealing with one county or part of a county only, or one region only; or where the subject is of local rather than national importance. Most archaeological papers are published in periodicals of this type.

(d) EPHEMERAL PUBLICATIONS (usually multigraphed or produced by other cheap methods of reproduction) are suitable for brief interim reports. During the last few years these publications have been developing and improving in quality. They often have specially designed covers which promote their sale. The increasing number of publications of this type is largely the result of the rising cost of conventional printing. Material of permanent value is being published in this manner to an increasing extent. None the less authors of papers are advised to try all other alternatives before resorting to this method.

(e) POPULAR PERIODICALS, such as *Antiquity*, *Archaeology* (U.S.A.), *Current Archaeology*, and the *Illustrated London News*, differ in function. *Antiquity* and *Archaeology* (U.S.A.), both quarterly, have tended to bridge the gap between the specialist and the well-informed general reader, bearing in mind that a specialist in one branch of archaeology is often a general reader in the rest of the subject. The *Illustrated London News* (now monthly) no longer contains such regular archaeological features as it did in the days of Sir Bruce Ingram (1877–1963), but it is still useful for reporting recent discoveries of importance.

(f) MISCELLANEOUS. Under this heading may be mentioned excavation reports and popular site guides published by the Directorate of Ancient Monuments, Department of the Environment; *ad hoc* publications by local authorities (e.g. the reports on the excavations in Winchester) including museums; monographs published by Universities, archaeological societies and smaller archaeological groups, and by private individuals. Examples include the *Archaeological Review* of Groups XII and XIII of the Council for British Archaeology, published by the University of Bristol; the *West Midlands Archaeological News Sheet* (Group VIII of the C.B.A.); and the *Reports of the Medieval Village Research Group*.

With this wide choice, almost any archaeological paper of reasonably good quality stands a good chance of being published somewhere.

The approach to the editor

Many archaeologists work in one county or two at most, and their medium for publication will most likely be the local archaeological periodical. They should join the local society and take part in its activities. Some of these societies have a rule against publishing material by non-members. In approaching the editor, care should be taken not to overestimate the length of the paper, as he may then decline it because it is expected to be too long, even before it has been written. It is just as important not to underestimate the length, as this throws out editorial calculations. It is desirable to check with the editor that the page size and shape of the volume are not about to be changed. This detail is important at the present time, as several archaeological societies have changed the format of their page from octavo to quarto within the last few years, and others may well follow this tendency. The advent of metric paper sizes is likely to lead eventually to further changes. Such changes affect the ratio of length to width of the illustrations, or the extent to which they should be reduced; the illustrations should therefore not be prepared until the format is known. It is also advisable to check with the editor that editorial policy follows the pattern of the immediately preceding volumes of the Society's publications. A new editor will often introduce a fresh policy.

Notes for guidance of contributors

Among the international and national periodicals which publish these valuable notes are:

American Journal of Archaeology, LXXIV (1970), 1–8; includes their recommended list of abbreviations;

Annual of the British School of Archaeology at Athens, XLIV (1949), 330–6, and supplement in LXV (1970), 277–80;

Archaeol. J. has 'Notes for guidance of contributors' at the end of each volume. They include a request that the mention of place-names be accompanied by their county or other ascription.

Britannia (the British annual volume of the Society for Roman Studies. I (1970), xiii–xiv.

Int. J. Naut. Archaeol. has 'Notes for Authors' at the end of each volume, including the request that 'authors should state on the title page their full name and postal address'.

Medieval Archaeol. supplies notes to intending contributors on request.

Numis. Chron. has 'Guidance for Contributors' at the end of each volume.

Post-Medieval Archaeol. supplies notes to intending contributors on request.

Proc. Prehist. Soc. has instructions to contributors at the end of the volume.

World Archaeol. has 'Notes to Contributors' at the end of each volume. Lettering on diagrams should be in the type-face UNIVERS (medium weight), obtainable on dry transfer sheets, e.g. Letraset and others. Each paper submitted should be accompanied by a summary.

The periodicals of county archaeological societies which have similar directives include:

Bedfordshire Archaeol. J., available on request from the editor.

Trans. Bristol Gloucestershire Archaeol. Soc., 'Notes for the Guidance of Contributors' at the end of each volume from 1973.

Proc. Cambridge Antiq. Soc., directions on inner back cover.

Trans. London Middlesex Archaeol. Soc., 'house rules' obtainable from the editor on request.

Montgomeryshire Collect., notes to contributors printed on inner front cover.

Trans. Shropshire Archaeol. Soc., notes for contributors among the preliminary pages of each volume.

N. Staffordshire J. Fld. Studs., information for contributors obtainable from the editor.

Wiltshire Archaeol. Natur. Hist. Mag., notes for contributors in LX (1965), 207–8.

Much can be learned by studying and comparing the requests made by the various editors. Recent directives show a growing tendency to ask contributors to submit their texts word-perfect so that they can be put straight into page proof, thereby saving the cost of galley proofs, and speeding production.

The study of other reports

The best preparation before drafting a report is to study other reports on the same subject, prepared by acknowledged authorities. One can learn 'how not to do it' from mediocre or bad reports, as well as 'how to do it' from first-class reports.

A select list of the latter is given in Appendix B. It is neither wise nor necessary to cite examples of the former.

For whom is the report written?

First of all, the report is intended to be read and understood by other people, and therefore it must be written as clearly and concisely as possible. It is likely to be read by all specialists concerned with the period, subject or locality with which it deals, and it will also most probably be read by a considerable number of non-professional archaeologists. As the vast majority of archaeological reports are published in the periodicals of archaeological societies, most of whose members are usually laymen, it should be intelligible to as many as possible of those members otherwise some of them will allow their subscriptions to lapse. Yet on the membership of the mildly interested laymen depends the very existence of these publishing societies. The present author, formerly Hon. Treasurer of one of the national archaeological societies for more than twenty years, received several resignations each year from members who gave as their reason the fact that they found the *Proceedings* of the society were becoming too 'highbrow'.

It has been pointed out that an author of any report, who does not consider the general run of those for whom he is writing it, 'is in great danger of writing to a mirror image of himself' (Shearing & Christian, 1965, 31).

All readers will consult the illustrations, and these will often be the only part of the report understood by foreigners; the importance of the illustrations is therefore self-evident.

When to prepare the report

A good archaeologist will have the structure of the report in his mind while doing his excavation, fieldwork, or other research. A report on an excavation should be finished within twelve months of completion of the excavation unless it was exceptionally large, when two years might be permissible. As it normally takes about a year for a long report to pass *via* an editor through the printer, it is reasonable to aim at publication within three years, at most, of completion of the excavation. As the major difficulty with excavation reports is to get in the specialist reports or appendices, these should be put in hand at the earliest opportunity. It is well to bear in mind that the 'top expert' is often too busy to receive another commitment, but he often does so without realizing that he may not be able to discharge it by any reasonable deadline. Therefore it is often far better to get a specialist report done by a perhaps younger person who is not already too heavily committed; there is then much more chance of his achieving the work by the deadline which should be supplied to him.

Shining examples of prompt publication are Sir Flinders Petrie, who kept up publication within about a year of completion of the excavation for about sixty years; and H. St. George Gray who did the same within a year or two of completing each excavation for about fifty years. There have been several excellent examples in recent years, e.g. Prof. Barry Cunliffe's reports on his excavations in *Roman Bath* (1969), and that by Geoffrey Wainwright and Ian Longworth (1971) on the complicated sites at *Durrington Walls*.

In one or two Scandinavian countries there is a law to the effect that the results of all archaeological excavations not published within five years of completion of the excavation become public property.

There is perhaps not quite the same urgency with publication of reports on external fieldwork or research on museum material, but it is still advisable to achieve publication as soon as possible, if only to 'get in first' in case a paper is being done on the same subject by someone else.

The need to prepare more than one copy

The writer should type a top copy and at least one, preferably two or three, carbon copies of his report. Copies can also be made by the Xerox system: this is particularly useful if the top copy has been amended extensively without the carbon copies having been altered. Line-drawings can be copied at little cost by photostat or any similar process.

Quite a number of archaeologists (and others) have written a report or even a whole book, and lost it by leaving it in the train, or had it stolen from their car, or it has been destroyed by a fire in their home, at the editor's or at the printers, or it has been lost during house removal. Such disasters can be avoided if more than one copy is made, *so long as a spare copy is kept in a different place*, a reasonable distance away from the original. It is useful to have third and fourth copies which can be lent to colleagues for comment or revision. Some publishers now require two copies of a typescript, to enable the printer to work on one for estimating the cost, while the editor works on the other, thus speeding production.

Clarity of style and freedom from jargon

Even to-day, there are many archaeologists who appear to write their reports on the assumption that to be 'scientific', it is necessary to load each sentence with long and technical words and to punctuate the narrative by footnote references to publications in as many foreign languages as possible; the more obscure the languages, the more 'scientific' the paper, notwithstanding that the author will frequently have misspelled words in those languages, thereby betraying his own ignorance of them to better-informed readers. On the other hand the author should not hesitate to quote relevant foreign parallels where necessary.

Papers should be written concisely in plain English, and 'padding', verbiage, and circumlocutions should be avoided; e.g., write 'because' or 'since' instead of 'in view of the fact that'. The present writer always tries to eliminate circumlocutions when moving from preliminary to final draft. It is good to submit one's report to an expert in good English who knows little or nothing about archaeology.

Note must be taken of the emergence of styles of writing, even perhaps a new language, consequent upon the development of newer disciplines in archaeology, including applications to our subject of new methods of analysis (e.g. D. L. Clarke, 1968 and 1972), the techniques of geographical location analysis (e.g. Fleming 1971 and Newcomb 1968 and 1970), and mathematical techniques (e.g. Hodson and others, 1971). Writers of these new types of archaeological report have a special duty to express themselves in plain English, and to define any unusual terms used, especially those which are not in the dictionaries.

Progress from preliminary to final draft

Most writers achieve their most worthwhile results by making two or three carbon copies of their first draft and lending them to their colleagues for their criticism. Lone workers can derive almost equal benefit by putting a first draft aside for a week or two and then revising it. In the case of long papers, it is the present writer's policy to prepare a first draft, and develop a second version a few weeks or even months later, adding fresh information and ideas and improving phraseology. Inexperienced writers will probably find it necessary to repeat this process with even the second version, before being in a position to prepare a third draft, which should if possible be final. Very few authors are able to produce a satisfactory text at the first attempt. What is easy to read has often been difficult to write.

Typing the report

Papers should be typed in double or triple spacing on one side of the paper only and on sheets of the same size, numbered consecutively. At present most editors and printers prefer large post quarto paper (255 mm by 204 mm) to foolscap as it is much easier to handle. However, the advent of metric paper sizes will eventually lead to the adoption of size A4 when the non-metric sizes become difficult to obtain. A margin of about 3 cm. wide on the left side and similar margins at top and bottom will enable the editor to make any corrections or directions for the printer. It is also advisable not to run too near the right hand margin.

The summary

More than a thousand papers on British archaeology alone are published annually, and it is a full-time job to read them all. It is therefore becoming customary for papers – especially those exceeding about twenty pages in length – to start with a summary of what the report is about; this looks well if printed in italics. A length not exceeding 200 words is recommended except for reports of exceptional length. Great care should be taken over this summary, as it will be more widely read than the rest of the report. Some writers and editors prefer to put this at the end, when the evidence on which the conclusions are based has been stated.

It is essential that this summary *be* a summary and not (as it tends to be in one or two periodicals) a background or introduction to what follows.

The abstract

In 1968 the Council for British Archaeology began publishing *British Archaeological Abstracts*, which at present appears twice annually. Its purpose is to keep archaeologists up to date by drawing their attention to recent work *of significance* in each period from palaeolithic to A.D. 1600, with more limited cover of post-medieval material. It is therefore not intended to summarize every paper published, and in general it omits those of a routine type. If an author makes a really adequate summary of his paper, stressing its main archaeological implications, that should normally form the basis for the *abstract* needed by the C.B.A., which would emphasize points of special interest, particularly what is new in the national context, and eliminate the routine detail.

Summaries done by authors of papers vary so much in length and emphasis that they do not necessarily provide a satisfactory basis for the *abstract* needed by the C.B.A. Some require expansion and others need a change in emphasis. Almost any paper on an area of overlap between archaeology and another discipline, if summarized by an author concerned mainly with the other discipline, will most likely require to be summarized with a different slant for *British Archaeological Abstracts*.

Readers will find it instructive to compare *British Archaeological Abstracts* with the recently launched *Polish Archaeological Abstracts*, vol. 1 of which (in English) appeared in 1972 and covers papers published in 1968 and 1969. Its chronological range is from palaeolithic to the fourteenth century A.D. It is available in the library of the Society of Antiquaries of London.

Archaeologists in the U.S.A. are similarly served by *New World Archaeology Abstracts*, and the *Surveys and Bibliographies* issued by their Council for Old World Archaeology (COWA).

The introduction

The content of this section depends largely on the character and subject-matter of the report. If it is of an excavation it should mention:

(a) The precise location of the site, with national grid reference (if in the United Kingdom) and name of the parish in which it is situated;

(b) the circumstances of discovery, reasons for excavation, and previous work on the site;

(c) the history of the site, beginning with its geology and continuing with references in documents and printed sources (see below);

(d) the condition in which the site has been left.

The following details should also be given, preferably in the form of one or more footnotes:

(e) The name(s) of the persons and/or societies carrying out the work;

(f) acknowledgments of financial or other assistance received, including matters such as the loan of shed, tools, etc.;

(g) the museum or collection where the finds are or will be deposited;

(h) the museum or library where the records of the excavation (or other field-work), including colour-slides and unpublished monochrome photographs, are to be or have been placed.

For (c), the previous history of sites excavated, one cannot do better than study the relevant portions of H. St. George Gray's excavation reports in *Proc. Somerset Archaeol. Natur. Hist. Soc.* between 1900 and 1950, which are particularly thorough. Accounts should include first of all the geology both solid and drift; all previous references in Anglo-Saxon charters, medieval and later documents including early maps such as estate maps and tithe maps; all previous printed references of any importance; the study of the local place-name and field names; and any evidence from air-photographs, whether vertical R.A.F. photographs on the scale of 1:10,000 or vertical or (more often) oblique views taken by Prof. J. K. St. Joseph or anyone else. The previous history of the site should be fully studied *before the excavation begins* and not as a subsequent afterthought, as it will almost certainly affect the planning of the excavation.

The compilation of a bibliography relating to the site or subject can be facili-tated by consulting Gomme (1907), which covers archaeological papers published in periodicals from 1665 to 1890. From 1891 to 1900 there are the annual biblio-graphies published by the Congress of Archaeological Societies. The period from 1901 to 1933 is covered by Mullins (1968). Publications between 1934 and 1939 are listed in the *Antiquaries Journal* for those years. The Annual Bibliographies issued by the Council for British Archaeology cover the years from 1940 to date. The Romano-British and Anglo-Saxon and (Christian) Celtic Bibliographies by Bonser (1957, 1964) are also extremely useful. It should however be noted that all these bibliographies concentrate on the periodical literature and only exceptionally do they include books. Finally, the topographical and subject card catalogues at the Society of Antiquaries of London, Burlington House, Piccadilly, London W1V 0HS, should be consulted to ensure that nothing has been overlooked. Those who are not Fellows of the Society should bring a letter of recommendation from a Fellow.

Acknowledgments

These are usually placed either near the beginning or at the end of the report – preferably near the beginning, for those whose help has been acknowledged will then receive an initial sense of satisfaction and may even be induced to read the rest of the report. The more important acknowledgments should appear in the text. These should start with a graciously worded appreciation of the kindness of the landowner and tenant for permitting the excavation; and follow with suitable thanks to those who lent major items of equipment; those who did the geophysical and other surveys; the photographers and those who drew the plans and sections; the illustrators of the finds; and the experts who assisted on the geology, docu-mentary sources, literary references, and produced the specialist reports. It is most important that no helper who has given appreciable assistance be omitted. The writer should avoid trying to give his text an air of authority by making acknow-ledgments to the great while ignoring help received from others.

With regard to the volunteers, they can either be covered by a general acknow-ledgment with a mention by name of the few who were particularly useful, or they can be specified individually, but if the list is long it should be relegated to a footnote. Any people who gave minor help such as lending tools can also be mentioned in a footnote.

Footnotes

Most editors like to have these double-spaced and on separate sheets. Care should be taken not to use terms such as op. cit., loc. cit., ibid., id., more than 1,000 words after the mention of the full titles of the works to which they refer. The modern tendency is *not* to set these in italics.

A provisional rough-out of the theme of the report

Although several authors including Philip Rahtz recommend that the illustra-tions be done before the report is written, some excavators find it convenient to start by producing a first rough-out of the text, perhaps not much more than three or four pages long, giving their preliminary ideas on the form that the report should take. This will help them to draw up an adequate list of illustrations related as closely as possible to the full text which will in due course be written.

3

THE BODY OF AN EXCAVATION REPORT:
THE ILLUSTRATIONS

David Price Williams

> It is evident how proper engravings are to preferve the memory of things, and how much better an idea they convey to the mind than written defcriptions, which often not at all, oftener not fufficiently, explain them.
> W. STUKELEY, *Itinerarium Curiosum*, 2nd edn (1776), preface

In any archaeological report, from the humblest preliminary paper to a five-volume final report, the same basic principles of illustration obtain. Since excavation is destructive and the moments of proof ephemeral, it is vital to record these moments as fully and as accurately as possible so that interpretation of the evidence can later be revised, and if necessary re-worked. Written descriptions are, however, often tedious and complex, making even simple stratigraphic problems sound like some geophysical manual. It is, moreover, sometimes impossible to convey in words how things looked during an excavation and no list of measurements will alone convey what was found – an excellent example of this would be the Sutton Hoo ship burial; hence, the use of illustrations is imperative. Illustrations are as much a part of the report as the text, but like a bad choice of words or the publication of endless, uninformative detail, illustrations can be misleading and are often published to no advantage.

Two points, then, should be borne in mind: *no* report should be published without illustrations; the illustrations should primarily inform, but may also enhance.

There are two classes of illustration:

(i) BLACK AND WHITE LINE DRAWINGS. These comprise maps, plans, sections, diagrams, drawings of pottery, flints, and other small finds, graphs, reconstructions, etc. These are all produced by black ink lines on a white background. They have no greys or other colouring.[1] The finished result is produced by the printer on a line block, and the cost is thus quite low. These will be the figures (Figs.).

[1] For a method of producing a grey tone by dotting or stippling, see Chapter 6.

(ii) PHOTOGRAPHS, USUALLY HALF-TONE. These normally show site views, excavated detail, objects of great aesthetic value or intricacy. It is always possible that colour photographs might be included, but this is at present unlikely. Black and white half-tone photographs are therefore generally used, but these are expensive to reproduce. They will be the plates (Pls).

By far the greatest number of illustrations will be line drawings. Photographs should be kept to a minimum, both because of the expense involved and because oddly enough they are not as useful as drawings, for they cannot convey actual size so easily, and frequently the lighting of the picture will not pick up all the necessary detail (but see pp. 52–56). Many captions to published photographs ought to read, 'Although not clear from the photograph . . .'.

Line Drawings

As the excavation proceeds, arrangements should be in hand not only to record the evidence but also to publish the records. The possibility that line drawings will be a necessary part of the report should be considered by the excavator before he has completed the excavation. It is hoped that there will be someone available who can draw archaeological illustrations for publication. It is important to realize that one does not have to possess artistic skill for many of the drawings since they are intended to depict the evidence rather than be a work of art.

Finished or publication drawings will almost certainly be copies of the relevant field or object drawings and will be in ink and not pencil. The drawings are scientific records and not thumbnail sketches, and therefore require careful production and proper equipment. The simplest outfit will include scale rules, compasses, dividers, set squares, T-square and board, and a set of drawing pens. The simplest pens to use are the Rotring Rapidograph range of the 'Variant' type with the non-blot offset nib. A typical range of sizes would be 0.8, 0.6, 0.4 and 0.2. These pens provide a constant width and constant density of line when used with the correct ink. Some draughtsmen prefer the Graphos pens, but the Rapidograph pens are easy to use and relatively foolproof if kept clean and held upright. An ordinary mapping pen is needed when lines of varying thickness are required.

There is, of course, a wide range of possibilities in deciding what material to draw on. In recent years there has been a move towards the use of plastics (polyester drafting film) such as Permatrace or Herculene, particularly for use in the field. This material combines stability – it neither shrinks nor stretches – with extreme durability in all conditions, wet or dry. It does not tear, and it can even be washed without any damage. For fieldwork it is one of the great aids to combat the wet or sweat that have ruined many good drawings. But these materials are not 'finishing' papers, despite what the instructions sometimes suggest. Unless special etching ink (such as Pelikan T or TT) is used, ink lines on plastic film will be of uneven density, may take a long time to dry, and tend eventually to flake off. The net result is a poor line block. Final drawings should be made on a prepared paper, heavy duty tracing paper at worst, though sheet drawing paper is preferable. This is a properly dressed paper such as Albanene (marketed by K. & E. and available from J. H. Steward Ltd., St. Catherine Street, London, WC2), although this particular one is expensive. The advantage of such paper is that it is designed to accept ink.

Most drawings will require lettering, if only in the title. Despite the apparent novelty and ease, handwritten lettering is rarely successful and if poorly done can detract from the appearance of the best scientific work. Three courses are then open:

(i) THE PRINTER may agree or even insist upon adding the lettering himself to a given specification. This is unusual, but if it is done, the titles and words are simply pencilled in place on the ink drawing and the printer will follow these. The result must then be checked carefully to ensure that this has been done correctly.

(ii) DRY PRINT LETTERING. This is a plastic transfer lettering which is rubbed into place from a backing strip. The two main firms supplying it are Letraset and Blick Dry Print. (Catalogues are available on request, together with the name of your nearest supplier, from either Letraset, 195 Waterloo Road, London SE1, or Blick Ltd., 116 Lordship Lane, East Dulwich, London SE22.) With dry print lettering the result should have a professional appearance, but great care must be taken to ensure accuracy of spacing. The variety of type faces (shapes) and points (sizes) is bewildering; for archaeological line drawings it is best to avoid fancy and 'bold' type faces. A 'Roman' typeface, such as Times New Roman, or a simple sans-serif face such as Univers, is as good as any. As for size, care should be taken to avoid using large type which can frequently dwarf the drawing. Light guidelines should be ruled in pencil before starting.

(iii) STENCILLING. The most preferable method of lettering is the use of a plastic stencil and ink pen. Standardgraph and Rapidograph both produce a comprehensive range of direct stencils, but the most effective system is the Leroy Offset stencil. The stencils and the scriber, which are initially expensive, can be obtained from J. H. Steward as above. The modern automatic nibs will fit into the Rapidograph range. With practice Leroy lettering is faster, neater and more effective than any other form.

The following points concerning draughtsmanship should be noted:

1. The drawing should first of all be sketched lightly in a fairly soft pencil to get the general spacing and proportions right.

2. The pen-and-ink work should be done, as far as possible, by working from top left to bottom right in order to avoid smudging work already done.

3. If additions or alterations are made, care must be taken to protect work already done by placing a sheet of paper between the hand and the drawing surface, especially if it is plastic sheet. Finger-marks can be removed from plastic sheet by the use of French chalk or 'pounce'.

35

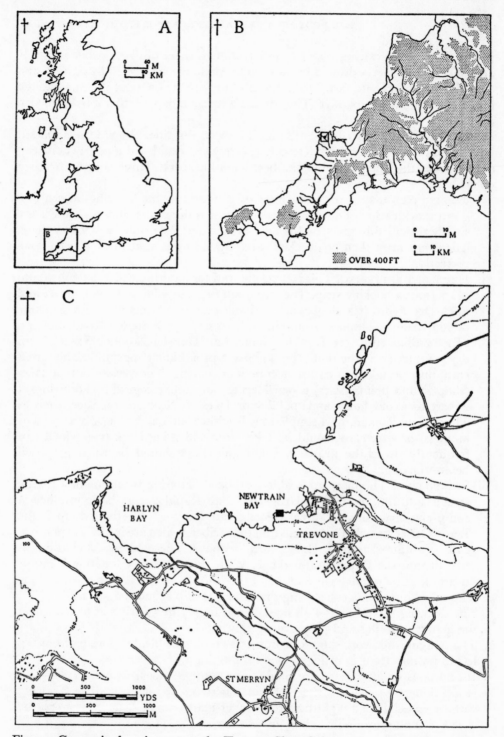

Fig. 1 Composite location map—the Trevone Slate Cairns
(Reproduced from the Ordnance Survey Map with the sanction of the Controller of
Her Majesty's Stationery Office, Crown copyright reserved)

4. For good reproduction, all lines whether heavy or fine should be drawn uniformly black. All pencil lines should be erased.

5. For corrections, Snopake is a quick-drying and non-cracking material to cover errors, but is highly inflammable. A better corrective is Process White paint which is photographically pure white.

6. Reduction (unless overdone) will always improve a drawing. It is therefore normal practice to produce the drawing between twice and four times the linear dimensions of the published result. Frequently a re-drawn tracing of the field drawing may be a suitable size to offer to the editor; it saves a great deal of time if the scale of the field drawing is decided with this in mind. On the extent of reduction that a drawing will bear, see Hope-Taylor (1966).

7. In such reduction lines reduce in thickness as well as in length. Furthermore, reduction decreases the white spaces between the lines, so the drawing should be 'open', otherwise the line block may 'fill in'. A reducing-glass is useful for checking on line-thickness after reduction. After a drawing has been done, it is well to have it photographed and reduced to the size intended in the publication; weak lines or other blemishes can then be corrected before the block is made.

8. As archaeological drawings are often produced over a fairly long period, it is good practice to write at the bottom of each drawing, as soon as it has been completed, a pencilled draft of the caption which it is intended to bear.

9. Pens, nibs, rulers, stencils, and other materials should be thoroughly washed in special cleaning fluid after use.

Maps (see also Chapter 6)

The principle of the map is to relate the relative positions of different places; there are normally three types of map that are required to explain the site being published. These can be known collectively as the *composite location map*, and it is now standard practice, at any rate in British archaeology, to combine these to fill a page (Fig. 1A, B, C).

(a) AN OUTLINE GENERAL MAP, on a small scale, showing the site in relation to the country as a whole, or to a major part of it.

(b) A MEDIUM SCALE MAP, showing rivers and contours, with the main hill masses indicated by shading or stippling within the contours. The site to be described should be boldly marked, and other sites of the same type or period in the region may be shown.

(c) A LARGE SCALE MAP, showing the site in its immediate environs. This will often be based on the Ordnance Survey 1:10,560 (6 inches to the mile) or 1:2500 ($2\frac{1}{2}$ inches to the mile) sheets. If it is based on maps published more than fifty years ago, no copyright fee is involved; otherwise it is necessary to resolve the copyright situation by applying to the Publication Division, Ordnance Survey, Romsey Road, Maybush, Southampton SO94 DH (see p. 86).

In order to ensure good reproduction, it is normal practice to redraw the appro-

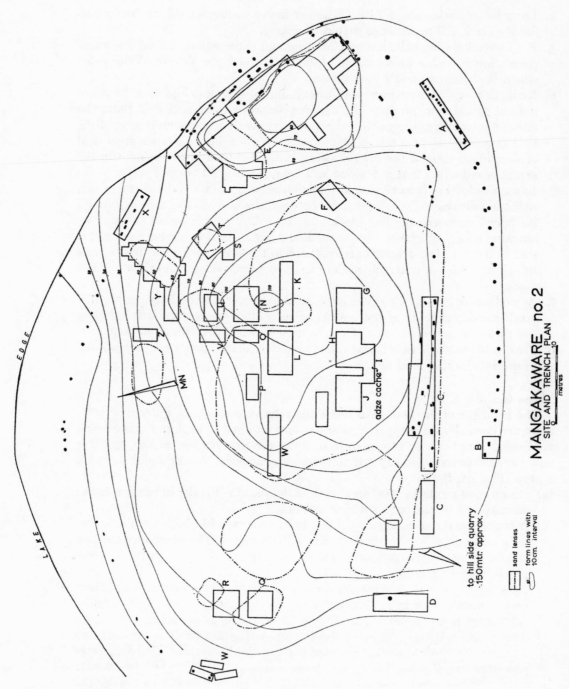

MANGAKAWARE no. 2
SITE AND TRENCH PLAN

to hill side quarry
.150mtr. approx.

sand lenses

form lines with
10cm. interval

Fig. 2 Site plan showing the excavated areas suitably anotated with letters, including scale and North point, though a little unclear

priate portions of these maps by tracing, at the same time omitting any details that have no relevance to the immediate purpose. For standard features such as churches, railways and so on, it is customary to use the conventional signs normally employed by the Ordnance Survey, or similar signs, unless there is a compelling reason to the contrary. Each map (excepting perhaps the general one) should bear a North point and a metric scale.

A certain flexibility is proper regarding the composite location map. The general map can be omitted in a report on an extremely well-known site. With less well-known sites this map is more essential in national publications than in those of county and regional societies, whose members can be expected to know where-abouts their region is in relation to the rest of the country. However, the needs of foreign readers have to be considered as well.

THE SITE MAP should show all the trenches or excavated areas, their relation to one another, their orientation and their number. These trenches need be put in only in outline at this time, but no trench or sounding can be omitted. The virtue of the plan is that when the text speaks of a particular trench by name, the reader can relate this visually to the site and to the other trenches mentioned. An academic point is the distinction between a map and a plan. The Ordnance Survey draw this distinction somewhere between the 1:25,000 *map* and the 1:10,560 (6 inches to the mile) *plan*. Most archaeological site 'maps' are therefore strictly site plans. (Fig. 2)

All maps and plans must have a title, usually the site and the year, thus: TIMBUKTU, 1972. They must also have a metric scale whatever other scale is included. In Egyptology for example, where the length of the ancient Egyptian cubit is known, the cubit scale is more meaningful than any other. The North point should if possible point to the top of the sheet.

Plans (Fig. 3)

The plans (other than the site plan just described) will show the detail of features within a trench, the relationship of walls to one another, the position of pits, hearths, ditches, robbed areas, etc. They will be the measured drawings which contain the stone-for-stone representation of the site. The field drawings, either taken from the site notebook or made by a surveyor on the site, will probably have been produced at a scale of 1:20 or 1:50. For publication they are traced off the field plans. The quality of the finished plan will of course depend upon the quality of the original field drawing, but there are a number of things that can be done to improve the appearance of the drawing for publication.

The usual fault with a field drawing is that it is cluttered with detail, no doubt with good reason. An attempt should be made to tidy this version up so as to make the final drawing more pleasing. The essential walls, for example, can be ac-centuated by being outlined more heavily. Features which cannot be readily interpreted by the excavator, such as patches of unrelated tumble or debris, can be minimized by drawing in such detail very lightly, say 0.2 in the Rapidograph

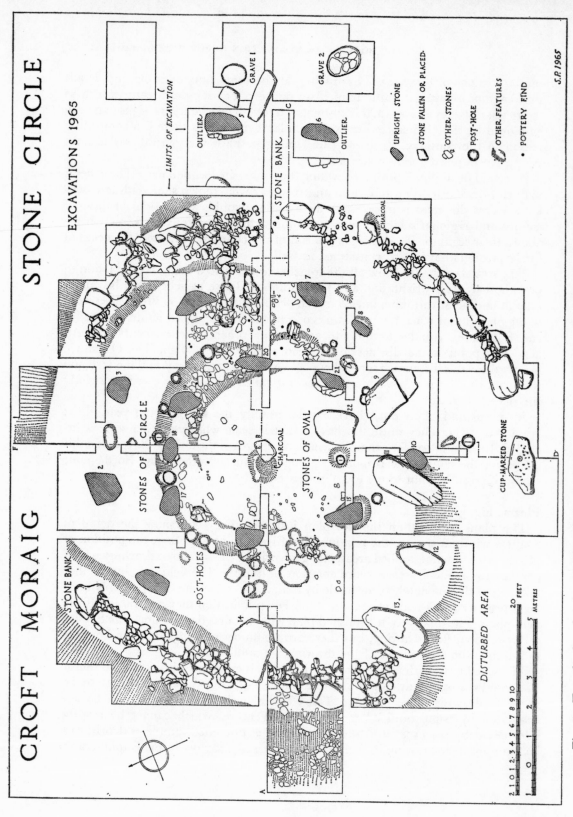

CROFT MORAIG   STONE CIRCLE

EXCAVATIONS 1965

LIMITS OF EXCAVATION

GRAVE 1

GRAVE 2

OUTLIER

OUTLIER

STONE BANK

STONE BANK

STONES OF CIRCLE

STONES OF OVAL

CHARCOAL

CHARCOAL

POST-HOLES

DISTURBED AREA

CUP-MARKED STONE

■ UPRIGHT STONE

▢ STONE FALLEN OR PLACED.

⬭ OTHER STONES

○ POST-HOLE

⬳ OTHER FEATURES

• POTTERY FIND

S.P.1965

Fig. 3   Trench plan showing the detail of an excavated area. Notice how the different stones can easily be picked out

range. The use of different line widths can easily bring a plan into focus and make the buildings stand out from the background, or vice versa.

Naturally there are many ways of drawing individual features. A wall, for example, may be shaded or even totally blacked in so that it will stand out on the page. Unless the scale will mean that the detail will disappear, however, by far the best way of showing any feature is to draw it as it was in the field, with a wall stone by stone. Ashlar masonry can be improved by ruling the outlines of the stones; a boulder and rubble wall is best drawn by hand. A simple trick to increase the apparent visibility of a wall is to outline the wall thickly, using Rapidograph 0.8 or 0.6 for the edges, and then draw in the interior detail of the wall lightly, with Rapidograph 0.4. This will make the wall stand out boldly. Extraneous detail can then be added at Rapidograph 0.2. The same technique may be used to make a circle of stones stand out from a whole field of stones. As for pits and ditches, these should be hachured according to the standard convention.

Although often attempted, the practice of giving only one trench plan for a multi-period site with four or five phases is never very successful and certainly not pleasant to look at. The usual technique is to represent each phase by differential shading, with a dated key at the side of the plan. This is no substitute for a plan of each phase, and should be used only as an adjunct to a complete set of phase plans. (For examples of plans showing periods or phases, see Wheeler 1943, 17, Fig. 3; Frere 1964, Figs. 2, 3, and 4; and Rahtz 1964, Fig. 18; that by Wheeler illustrating six successive phases on the same page, thereby facilitating comparison.)

As with maps, all plans require a title, a metric scale and a North point, preferably pointing to the top of the sheet.

Sections (Fig. 4)

The section is intended to add the third dimension to the trench plans. As such, the section and the plan should always be cross-referenced, either by using a–a, b–b notation on the plan, or by calling the section 'West Baulk, Trench 11a, North–South' or by some such title.

In the past, some reports have managed to stagger into the light of day without sections; this is like trying to learn a foreign language without a dictionary. The whole presentation of the excavator's stratigraphic analysis and hence his interpretation of the site has depended upon his sections; so they stand as the only record of that interpretation. Normally one cannot publish every section of a site ever drawn in the field, and would choose only those which do not duplicate one another and that are instructive and relevant to the text. If, however, there is to be any error of number, it should be in favour of too many sections, not too few.

Methods of drawing sections vary widely. The main methods are the naturalistic, the stylistic, and a compromise between them. The classic example of the naturalistic section is Bersu, 1940. The stylistic method is followed in most modern excavation reports. These methods are compared by Wheeler (1954), 59–61, and more recently by Barker (1969), Biddle and Biddle (1969), and Coles (1972), 203–5.

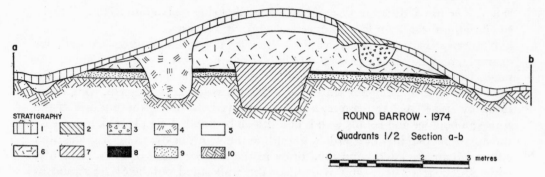

Fig. 4 Two methods of drawing sections
(a) A stylistic notation with a key. The numbers of layers might also have been inserted on the section itself

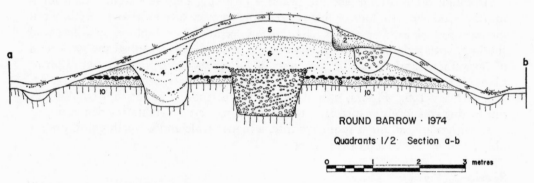

(b) A more naturalistic section

If drawn stylistically, the junctions between layers in a section are usually marked by continuous lines. These junctions are often not shown in the sections drawn on the compromise and naturalistic methods. The subsoil is often shown by a thick line, but practice in this respect is not uniform.

The field sections, probably on graph paper but if at all possible on plastic sheet backed with graph paper, will usually be at a scale of 1:10 or 1:20. Obviously the most desirable thing to do would be to publish the plans and the sections at the same scale. Unfortunately this is rarely done, nor is it often practicable. The vertical interval of the section is usually quite small but the detail is often intense; that is to say that many layers which are no more than a few mm. thick in the field have to be represented in the publication. The detail can only then be obtained by making the drawings large. In many cases the excavator is going to have to consider publishing his sections on folded sheets, though this practice should be avoided if at all possible.

The section should be traced from the field drawings, first by tracing in the skeleton, the main dividing line of the section and the two ends. (This is always assuming that clear divisions between layers were visible in the field, which is not invariably the case.) At this point comes the vexed question of conventions – how are the layers to be filled in? Should each layer be shaded in a different way, inventing more and more complex geometric symbols for the distinction between, say, 'bricky ash' and 'ashy brick', or should one try to draw a representation of what is present – 'brick debris' being drawn as pieces of brick and associated matter, 'sandy' being dotted more or less depending upon the degree of sandiness? The problem here is to decide what to do with 'sterile fine earth', though one must be ready to leave some layers as white spaces, which assist clarity.

Examples of different conventions are to be seen in Atkinson 1953, 199, or in Webster 1964, 148–52. There is no fixed principle on the finishing of sections, but there are certain points which should be borne in mind. If conventions are used to excess, the overfilled section will become so cluttered as to be jarring to the eye and so less instructive. Those conventions which are used should be light (Rapidograph 0.2) and sparing, bearing in mind the reduction to come. If there is a doubt as to whether a layer should be shaded or not, it is always better to have too few layers with shading conventions than too many.

All sections should be fully titled and cross-referenced to the plan; they should have a metric scale and also some reference to the direction (a North–South section might have N. and S. at the appropriate ends to avoid further confusion). All layers should be numbered strictly in accordance with the text numbers and not the field numbers should they be different. Similarly, walls and other features referred to in the text might well appear in the section and should be numbered. If it so happens that a significant object, for instance a coin, appeared in the section, then this should be put in and labelled.

Occasionally, a section may have to be drawn, perhaps of a long narrow cutting, or a pipe-line trench, which if drawn up in one piece would be very long and thin – the section of a 40 m. test trench some 20 cm. deep! If published as one, it will look like a clothes line, and so it should be broken into a number of page-sized lengths which can then be referenced to one another.

For copyright and other reasons it is good practice for each map, plan, section, or reconstruction to bear the name or initials of the author, and the year.

Reconstructions (Figs. 5, 6)

Every excavator should try to visualize his site in three dimensions using axonometric or isometric drawings, and wherever possible it is good policy to include a conjectural reconstruction in a report. A good reconstruction is usually beyond the artistic competence of the excavator unless he is particularly talented in this direction, and a competent artist is often called in to undertake this work. An excellent book of archaeological reconstructions is that by Sorrell (1965). A list of archaeological reconstructions, arranged by period, is given as Appendix A.

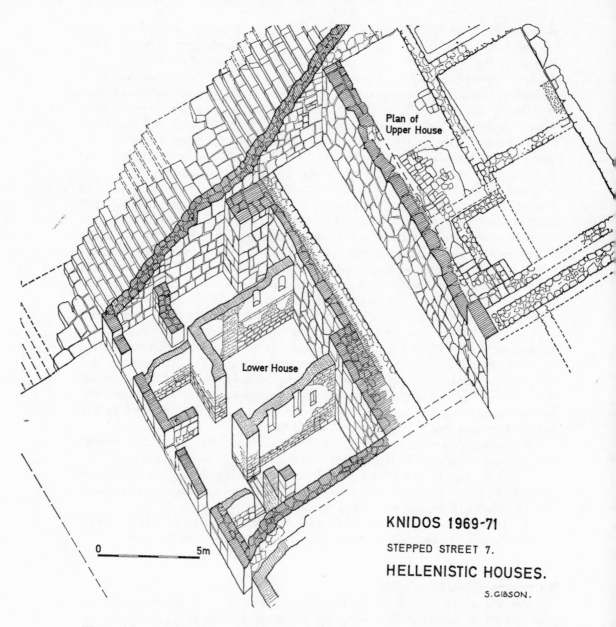

Plan of
Upper House

Lower House

0   5m

KNIDOS 1969-71

STEPPED STREET 7.

HELLENISTIC HOUSES.

S.GIBSON.

Fig. 5   An axonometric projection of excavated walls only. The essence of projection is that three-dimensional walls have all lines drawn to exact scale, which explains the distortion

Fig. 6 (opposite)   A hypothetical reconstruction, based upon the axonometric projection

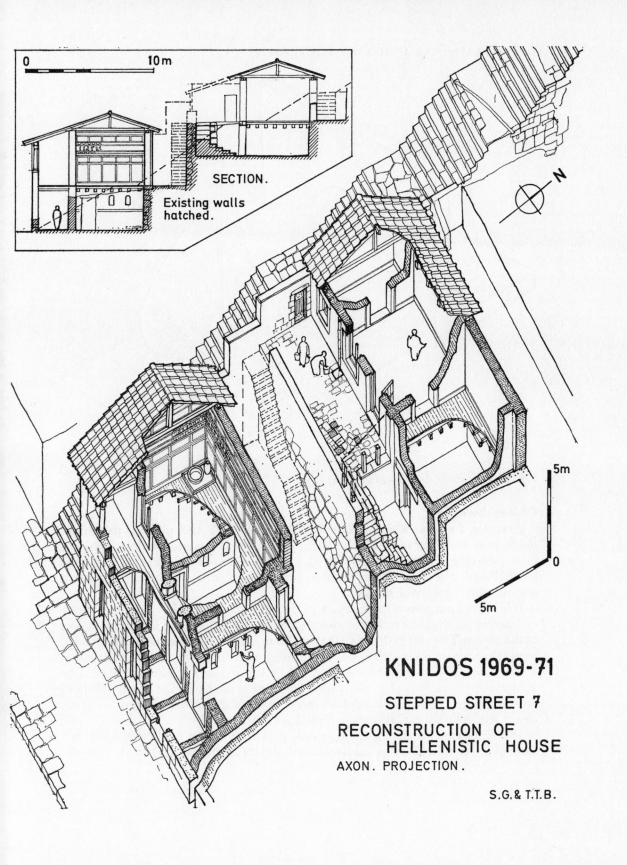

0   10 m

SECTION.

Existing walls
hatched.

5m

0

5m

KNIDOS 1969-71

STEPPED STREET 7

RECONSTRUCTION OF
HELLENISTIC HOUSE

AXON. PROJECTION.

S.G.& T.T.B.

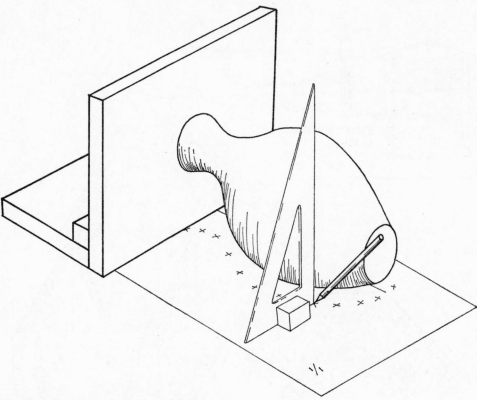

Fig. 7   One method of drawing a pot

Object drawing

POTTERY. In a site which is late Neolithic or Bronze Age, perhaps the largest single item for illustration will be pottery, with good fortune whole vessels, but more probably potsherds. Whilst only a small fraction of the excavated mass may be published, one may still expect page after page of pottery drawings which will indicate the typology of the site.

It is not the purpose of this chapter to give an exhaustive guide to the technique of drawing pottery, but rather to give a guide to the appearance of pottery figures in the report. The aim of drawing is to give a measured reproduction of the vessel, reconstructing where possible, but illustrating particularly the shape, decoration and section. Of necessity the drawing will be stylized and no attempt should be made at stark realism. Shading is used only where necessary for clarity. Only in certain cases should any attempt be made to show the surface texture. A clear, clean, stylized drawing, therefore, should be the aim.

The simplest method for drawing whole pots is to rest the pot horizontally on a sheet of paper against a vertical backboard, its rim flush with the board. With the aid of a vertically held set-square, or, better still, a set-square which has been blocked with wood to stand upright, salient points such as the rim, base, carinations (sharp changes in angle), and handle can be projected downwards on to the paper and the resulting dots joined up to give an accurate 1:1 outline of the pot. For rim sherds, the sherd should be placed with its rim on to the vertical board as before; sighting along the board whilst manipulating the sherd backwards and forwards will ensure that when no light appears between the rim and the board, the rim is at the correct angle. The outlining procedure is followed as above. The diameter can be reconstructed very easily by placing the rim as before on a series of concentric circles drawn on a separate sheet of paper until at the correct angle the rim accords with one of the circles. This distance having been measured on to the drawing the sherd profile can be traced off and drawn in reverse at the appropriate diameter. Base sherds can be done in the same manner. (Fig. 7)

Strict rules apply to the remainder of the process. All drawn pots will be divided in half by a vertical line from the centre of the rim to the base, or to the farthest extent of the pot in the case of a sherd. This line bisecting the drawing is the one edge of a cut-away quadrant, which the reader will envisage as he looks at the pot. To the left of the line he will see the inside of the pot and a section of the wall from the centre of the base; to the right will be only the outside with its appendages and decoration. All internal decoration, then, is shown on the left of the centre line. This decoration should be foreshortened the further left it is shown. At the left-hand edge will appear the caliper-measured section of the pot wall. To the right of the centre line all external decoration will be shown, again suitably foreshortened. Both inside and outside, lines of sharp change in angle are shown by ruled horizontal lines, as are the lines of the rim and base, at least in wheel-made pottery; the lines on hand-made pottery should be drawn freehand. Single handles are shown to the right of the drawing. A section through the handle will then appear to the right of the handle. Two-handled pots will have one handle on the right as an exterior view, and one on the left which will be seen cut vertically in half.

Of course so far all the drawings will be in pencil. The inking-in stage is the time to clean the drawing up and give it clarity. The same thickness of line should be used for all pottery drawings and should never vary. An indiscernible change in line thickness at 1:1 is paradoxically more obvious when reduced. The best thickness will be Rapidograph 0.6, apart from the section which will be blacked or shaded in on the left-hand side. Handle sections should also be blacked or shaded in, and the point of section marked on the drawing. Monochrome decoration can be shown in black, but polychrome, particularly involving red paint, should be shown with black shading. If the decoration on the shoulder of the vessel is not properly visible due to foreshortening of the full frontal drawing, then a separate addition should be made above the pot by drawing two concentric partial circles and the decoration reproduced as if it were on a flat surface. Internal or external centre decoration should be placed within a separate circumference directly above

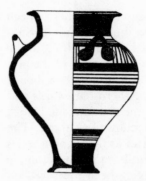

Fig. 8 Decorated pot. Three-handled Mycenaean vase—the outer decorated surface is shown on the right; the undecorated interior is on the left. Vertically repetitive decoration should be foreshortened towards the profile. Reproduced 1:4

or below the vessels as the case may be. Plastic or incised decoration should be shaded or stippled. (Fig. 8)

No reconstruction beyond that which can be measured should be attempted. The vessels or sherds should be shown as they are, not as the keen excavator thinks they might have been; nor is it a good practice to dot in a proposed reconstruction since this could be misleading. If an interpretation is made in the text, that may be all to the good, but the reader should have the opportunity to understand the evidence from which the interpretation has been made.

Having drawn all the necessary pots and sherds, the next job is to make up the figures. This is an easy task so long as the following points are remembered. The drawings are normally at 1:1 and can be expected to be reduced between 1:2 and 1:8, according to size of pot, type of decoration, and other considerations.

Unless exceptionally large or small pots are involved, one can think in terms of a general purpose reduction to 1:4 or 1:5. For reduction sizes in special cases see Case 1961, Longworth 1961, Myres 1969 and Clarke 1970. The reduction ratio should be decided first in consultation with the editor of the periodical in which the report is to be published.

The plate or figure size of the intended publication should be measured; this is not the page size but the size of the printed area within the margins. If this size is multiplied by the reduction ratio, and sheets of card or paper for mounting are cut to that size, the Plates (or Figures) when reduced will be the correct size for publication. (Fig. 9)

The drawings should be cut out individually leaving a small margin between them. In the interest of economy they should be mounted as close together as possible, leaving however enough space for insertion of numbers or letters. The drawings can then be stuck on to the backing paper with mounting glue such as Copydex, Jiffitex, or one of the other ammonium-based latex glues, which permit extraneous glue to be rubbed off easily. The arrangement of the drawings will depend on the agreed typological or locus order determined by the text. The rim lines of all the drawings should be parallel to the top of the page, and the centre lines if possible should be in a line one below the other. The temptation to fill gaps with irrelevant drawings should be overcome. Differences in the whiteness of the

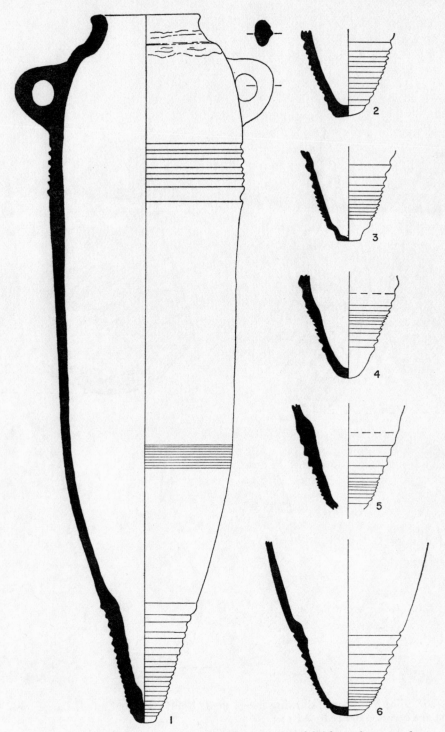

Fig. 9 The finished drawings reduced to 1 : 4, and laid out in a regular fashion on the page

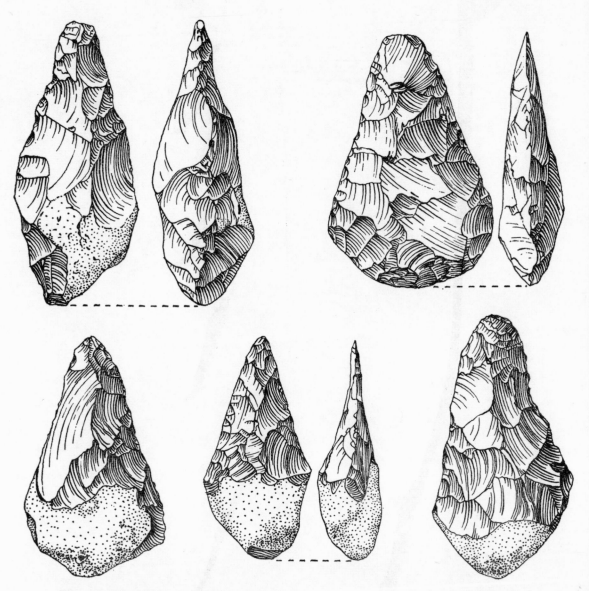

Fig. 10 Flint hand tools, showing facets shaded and cortex stippled. Large tools like these are occasionally reduced 1 : 3

background or apparent shadows of the outline of the paper will not affect the finished figure. The blockmaker will employ a high contrast technique which mercifully takes all the greys and creams to white, and all darks to black, which will give a shadow-free finish. An added bonus is that the reduction of the drawings will inevitably enhance them by making the errors smaller. A reducing glass can be used at the setting-up stage to emulate this effect if desired.

Each illustrated pot or sherd is lettered or numbered consecutively from top left to bottom right to link with the text, and the whole page is given a title and Figure number. Where there is more than one page of drawings of pots or sherds, the Figures will be numbered consecutively, and the pots individually numbered from 1 upwards on each Figure. Letters should be avoided since they are finite.

It is always easier to write the text when the Figures have been made up because it is the Figure number that will dictate the reference.

Those interested in additional artificial aids to pottery drawing may note the use of *sherd radii* (Trump 1971).

FLINT IMPLEMENTS AND FLAKES. Objects of flint are generally drawn in pencil and then inked in freehand with a fine nibbed pen such as a mapping pen. It is imperative that flints be drawn with lines of variable thickness and therefore with a pen with a flexible nib. The drawing size is usually 1:1, but the reduction to bear in mind is 1:2, although the French prefer 2:3. The dorsal view is usually sufficient, dorsal face visible, bulbar face underneath with the butt at the base and the distal end at the top. The artifact is outlined and then the facets or flaking ridges are added. Light semi-circular shading is then drawn within the flaking ridge. As with all three-dimensionally conceived drawings, the light source is imagined to be at the top left-hand corner of the paper. Whilst it is quite in order, then, to leave the left facets unshaded, it is not good to overshade the right facets. Reduction intensifies shading. (Fig. 10)

The normal convention for showing the cortex (the weathered surface of the original nodule) is by rough dotting. Polished facets are blacked in.

If a second view is thought necessary for significant pieces, the butt view is drawn below the dorsal view, percussion bulb down, and shaded accordingly. Sometimes a side view is also added alongside the dorsal view, for example with hand-axes, some scrapers, leaf points and certain other classes of artifact. The percussion bulb here is outwards. For examples of these conventions see Bordes (1968) and items listed in Appendix B, final section.

When making up the Figures, each object should be numbered separately and consecutively, all drawings of the same object under one number. The technique for making up is the same as for the pottery Figures. When the reduction is decided upon, it MUST be stated on each Figure of the finished publication. It is often expressed in the form of a ratio (1:3), but it is better to draw a metric scale on each page of illustrations; as this is reduced to the same extent as the drawings it can never be wrong providing that it is correct to begin with.

OTHER SMALL OBJECTS. The normal practice is to illustrate almost all small finds

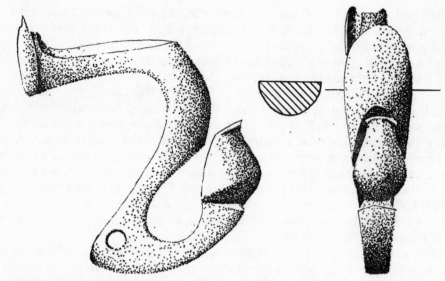

Fig. 11 Stippled dot technique. A side and frontal view of a copper fibula and a shaded section for metal (2:1)

except when a large number of the same type are found (such as the hoard of twelve tons of iron nails from Inchtuthil in Perthshire). Some objects are complicated and may require several drawings. A simple rule for the number required for each object is that the reader should be presented with as many views as are necessary to depict the shape and dimensions of the object without ambiguity. For example, a brooch might require both front and side view but an oblique view would add no additional information. Pins and nails require one view, head up, point down, with the addition of a section to the right of the drawing. This section should be marked on the drawing; it will show squareness or hollowness which will not be clear from the frontal drawing alone.

The drawings should be done in the first instance in pencil, usually at 2:1, that is to say, twice actual size. Sometimes it is necessary to draw three or even four times linear, and production of such enlarged drawings can be assisted by the use of mechanical devices such as the Variograph, or Kenrick's epidiascope (Kenrick 1971). Proportional dividers are also helpful in this context. The reduction will probably be of the order of 1:1 or 1:2, but the large size of the original will enable full advantage of the reduction to be taken.

Once the object has been drawn in pencil, it can be outlined with either a mapping pen or a Rapidograph 0.2. Every attempt should now be made to give the object a three-dimensional appearance, and this is done by shading. As with flints, the light source is located at the top left hand corner of the paper, and there are two equally popular conventions for darkening the areas in shadow.

The first is the dotted shading technique. Small dots (Rapidograph 0.2) are gradually added to the shadowed side (right) in ever-increasing numbers into the shadow until a three-dimensional appearance is gained. The less the shadow, the fewer dots are required. If this style is decided upon, however, the light dotting should first be applied over the whole shaded area, and then more dots added gradually over the top of this until the desired increase in density has been obtained. The temptation to dot heavily in the deep shadows must be watched. If done properly however, this style can produce spectacular results, giving a three-dimensional aspect of great clarity. The unshaded highlights in particular give a polish to the object. The major drawback to the dotting technique is that if it is carried to extremes, it can make a decayed and pitted metal terminal look like a brand new chromium-plated ball bearing. Very often, and especially for iron objects which tend to be heavily oxidized, this type of shading is far too formal and the highlighting too aggressive. On the other hand it is excellent for the more rounded features of bronze objects or stone carvings, and it is simple and effective for the less gifted artist. (Fig. 11) (Fig. 12)

The second method for darkening areas in shadow is the technique of hatching, using thin, imprecise and often broken semi-parallel lines over the shadowed area, gradually thinning the lines, increasing their distance apart and shortening them towards the highlights. Additional pecks, blobs and blotches can bring out the most heavily textured ironwork. Cross-hatching however, that is using lines at 45 degrees to one another, should be avoided as it usually looks rather scratched.

Four points are to be borne in mind when shading. First, to show the object as it is and not how it ought to be or how it might look best. The drawing is thus a record and not a work of art. Secondly, light shading is always better than heavy shading. Undershading will look well when reduced, but heavy shading will tend to look blotted. Thirdly, it is well to plan the shading of an object by pencilling-in the areas of shade before working them up in ink. Objects can have very complex shadows which take time to work out. Finally, it should always be remembered that the shading has to be drawn on the assumption that there is a source of light at the top left of it.

Any section of metal objects should be shaded and not blacked in.

Drawings of objects of bone should be shaded as lightly as possible as they are normally light in colour and have little contained shadow.

It is most unusual to have to draw skeletal bones. The system of written recording and measurement is so well understood that drawings of bones are scarcely ever published now, unless by an expert. Any abnormalities will be shown by X-rays or other photographs (Brothwell 1972).

Half-Tone Plates

It is customary to number these in large Roman capitals (I, II, III, and so on) to avoid confusion with the Figures (1, 2, 3, etc.). Selection of half-tones depends largely on the type of report, but restraint is recommended in view of their high cost of reproduction. They can be considered under the following headings:

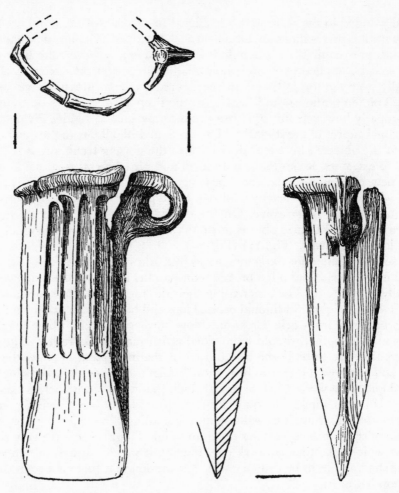

Fig. 12 Shading technique. The metal section shaded and the top view projected above the object (1 : 1)

I. **The early illustration**

It may happen that the site was drawn by one of the early antiquary-draughtsmen such as John Aubrey (1626–97); Edward Lhuyd (1660–1709); William Stukeley (1687–1765); William Borlase (1695–1772) who worked in Cornwall and Scilly; Rev. John Skinner (1772–1839) whose drawings are scattered among his hundred volumes of Journals in the British Museum; or Sir Henry Dryden (1818–99) whose collection of plans of archaeological sites in England is in Northampton Public Library. For Roman sites known since last century there are often unpublished drawings by Samuel Lysons (1763–1819). In the Lukis Museum in Guernsey are the drawings by members of the Lukis family, which cover prehistoric (especially megalithic) monuments in the British Isles as well as the Channel Islands. Drawings of this type occur in the libraries of many of our national and county archaeological societies. The inclusion in a report of a reproduction of such a drawing can add to the attractiveness of the report, especially if used as a frontispiece, and particularly if the report appears as a monograph, when such a frontispiece is likely to result in increased sales.

II. The general view

An *aerial photograph* of the site, taken either before or (usually better) during the excavation will almost always enhance the interest of the report. Oblique aerial photographs make the most attractive pictures, but vertical aerial photographs can be related more satisfactorily to maps and plans. A *ground photograph* of the site is desirable (a) if it is to be destroyed after being excavated; or (b) if the site is naturally photogenic, when inclusion of the photograph may increase the saleability of the report. Otherwise a general view would not seem to be essential if the information which it would reveal can be obtained more accurately from a plan based on the O.S. 1:10,560 or 1:2500 map.

III. Details of excavations

General views of the excavation are not necessary unless they provide more information about the site than the plans, or clarify points of detail not covered by the line drawings, or provide cogent evidence more convincingly than the line drawings, or illustrate some point of excavation technique. There must in any case be adequate reason for including each photograph, and one has only to glance through the numerous excavation reports in any periodical to note how many unnecessary photographs (often of poor quality) have been included where there was inadequate editorial restraint and guidance.

Whether included in the report or filed for reference, photographs of cuttings should all be compared with the drawn sections and in the event of inconsistencies the drawings must be amended as well as the excavator's interpretation. All photographs published must be of the first quality.

IV. Small finds

Most of these will have been illustrated by line drawings. The present tendency is for photography to be reserved, as far as possible, for objects of aesthetic quality, or of detail so intricate as to defeat all but the most experienced draughtsmen (who cannot always be obtained). It is also usual to reproduce ancient British, notable Roman, Anglo-Saxon and Medieval coins by photography. This may be done by either direct photography, or (in the case of shiny or discoloured coins) by photographing plaster casts, thereby eliminating the shine or discoloration.

The technique of preparing photographs

Archaeological photography is explained in books by Cookson (1954), Conlon (1973), Matthews (1968), and Simmons (1969). It is vital that archaeological sites and sections be adequately prepared for photography by being scrupulously tidied up beforehand in all instances. All photographs intended for publication should show good definition, and a fair (but not excessive) degree of contrast with detail visible in the shadows; they should be of reasonable size (at least half-plate), and certainly larger than the size of the block which is to be made from them. They should be printed 'black-and-white, glossy'.

The following photographic sizes should be noted:

Whole-plate: 16·5 cm. × 21·6 cm.
Half-plate: 12·1 cm. × 16·5 cm.
Quarter-plate: 8·3 cm. × 10·8 cm.

Photographs of sites or objects should nearly always include a scale, which must be neat, accurate, and unobtrusive. The use of objects such as shovels and coins as scales is to be deprecated. Photographs of objects of high aesthetic quality, such as some of the finds from Sutton Hoo, or the Alfred Jewel, or fine Celtic metalwork, usually omit any scale which would tend to disfigure the illustration; it is preferable to state the size of the object in the caption beneath.

Where photographs are to appear as page or half-page illustrations, they may be captioned by lightly *pencilling* on the back the title and plate number. Care must be taken to prevent any indentation of the face of the photograph from paper clips, writing too heavily on the reverse, or other causes. Where more than one object is to appear on the same plate and these objects have been photographed separately, it may be necessary to mount them as with drawings of pottery or small finds (see p. 49). In this case all the photographs should show the same degree of tone and the same background, usually white. Where backgrounds differ greatly in individual photographs to be mounted as a composite page, it may be as well to eliminate the background before mounting. Whatever procedure is adopted each object should then be lettered or numbered and separately listed under the main title for the plate.

When photographs are mounted in this way care should be taken to ensure that they are to the same scale. If not, the different scales should be clearly indicated on the titling. It is always wise to include in the text the measurements of photographed objects. With subjects to be reduced in size uniform scale of prints saves money in blockmaking, since all prints can be made into one block and cut to printed size, thus avoiding 'minimum' charges for individual small blocks.

Most photographs when taken contain superfluous marginal detail. This can be masked in one of various ways – by the use of a frame cut in paper, by appropriate indications in ink or pencil on the front or back of the photograph or, perhaps best of all, by shading the unwanted areas with chinagraph pencil (which can be easily rubbed off after the block has been made).

*   *   *

Processes of pictorial reproduction

Pen-and-ink drawings of maps, plans, sections, reconstructions and objects are usually reproduced by the 'line block' process; photographs usually by the 'half-tone' process. It is useful to visit a good printing or engraving firm to obtain a thorough understanding of these processes: this will be of great interest and value and save time in producing satisfactory work for the printer. The subject is covered by numerous publications, and usefully summarized by Wheeler (1954), 196–9.

Arrangement of illustrations for the editor

When the paper has been completed, the author should include at the front of his text a list of all illustrations, under the headings of *List of Figures* and *List of Plates*, giving number of illustration, caption, size, suggested degree of reduction, size when reduced and how this relates to the page size. Illustrations should as far as possible be multiples of page size to save wastage of space, or at least the long or short dimension should be a multiple of the page length or width. He should indicate where the illustrations should ideally be placed in the text.

Folders should be avoided wherever possible as they are expensive. If it is necessary to include many drawings which because of their detail have to be larger than page size, it may be easier to put the printed versions into a separate wallet at the back of the report or even in a separate box sold with the text (e.g. Phillips, 1970; Es, van, 1967).

If it is intended to publish the report as a monograph rather than to get it into one of the established periodicals, it will be possible to design the whole format including the size and shape of the illustrations. A mock-up can then be made of the whole report with photographic copies of the illustrations, and the printer can work from this. A report of this kind now being prepared by one of us (P.A.R.) is based on an A4 size format used *horizontally*, which is much more suited to most plans and sections than the vertical format into which nearly all reports published in the periodicals of archaeological societies have now to be straitjacketed.

If the editor is supplied with photographic reproductions of the illustrations, reduced to the sizes recommended by the author, his work as editor will be greatly facilitated, and risk of editorial damage to the original drawings will be minimized.

4

THE BODY OF AN EXCAVATION REPORT:
THE TEXT

Philip Rahtz

> To empty the contents of notebooks on a reader's head is not publishing. A mass of statements which have no point, and do not appear to lead to any conclusion or generalization, cannot be regarded as an efficient publication. (Sir) W. M. Flinders Petrie, *Methods and Aims in Archaeology* (1904), 50–51

The purpose of a report is to provide a record of the evidence destroyed during the course of excavation. This should be set out as clearly as possible to enable the reader to know at least what the excavator *thought* he had found. The report may and usually does also include the excavator's interpretation of what he thinks the evidence means; this is ultimately of less value than the evidence, but is more likely to be read than the data on which it depends (see Chapter 1).

Archaeological excavation is a non-repeatable operation, and the report should ideally record all the evidence which has been destroyed; it should include details of every relationship observed in the soil: of walls, ditches, pits, postholes, hearths, and floors, to the layers above and below them; and the position of every find. The completeness of a report is limited only by the cost of publication. In any case, it is wise to write the report very fully in the first draft; this can later be pruned for publication but a copy of the full draft should be deposited with the finds in the appropriate museum.

The ideal report in theory and practice

The ideal report would enable a reader to reconstruct the whole site layer by layer, feature by feature, each with its constituents such as clay, gravel, and charcoal flecks in due proportion; and in such a way that all finds and features such as walls and pits could be replaced or reconstructed in their original positions. From the written account with its plans, sections, details of content and character of soils, descriptions and illustrations of finds, a future archaeologist could mentally re-excavate and if necessary re-interpret the site; an example of this is the brilliant re-interpretation by Hawkes (1948) of the sites on Cranborne Chase excavated by Pitt-Rivers more than half a century previously.

Any gap between this ideal and its realization is evidence destroyed without record, and lost with the memory or death of the excavator. Such a complete record is, however, impossible to achieve in practice; no excavation would be completed if there were such minute dissection of every cubic centimetre of soil (though this statement may be proved wrong a century hence!). The publication would be too costly and too indigestible for its readers. Moreover, much evidence is lost even in the most careful excavation by the inadequacy of present-day applications of scientific techniques; these, though increasingly important to archaeology, are in their early stages of development. Evidence is lost to us now in the same way as early barrow-diggers missed much that can be recorded today, because of their lack of even the elementary scientific methods available now. The responsibility of a present-day excavator is therefore great if he is not to be a vandal. A research excavation should be done only after careful deliberation and if the fullest resources in the field and laboratory are available. Rescue excavations are easier to justify: any *reliable* evidence that can be salvaged from the plough and bulldozer is better than none.

Theoretically, the finds will be preserved for all time in the museum in which they are deposited. But they do sometimes get lost, or more commonly deteriorate through lack of conservation. In any case it may be difficult for most readers of a report to visit the museum. So the finds should be described and drawn fully in such detail that nothing else could be learned (except by new scientific techniques) by examining the finds themselves. They should be fully drawn and if necessary photographed in black-and-white, and where appropriate in colour. Details not apparent in the illustration should be given in the text, with a note on the material of which the objects are made. A practice which is gaining many adherents is to put as much information on the drawing as possible, to minimize or even eliminate the text. With pottery in particular, a coding system for such information as colour of glaze, part of pot, technique of decoration, etc. can be incorporated in the drawing (Smith 1970).

Scientific information must be accurate, whether it describes the kind of grits, clay and glaze of pottery, or the proportion of different metals, and the technique of construction, of a brooch.

In describing the evidence of molluscs, soils, or slags or in assessing the full evidence of objects, we must rely on the specialist, who may be a scientist or art historian. Their reports form an increasingly large part of a modern report, and are discussed later in this chapter.

The first duty of the excavator is to record the evidence and this may be all that a beginner may achieve in his first reports. But attempts should be made to clothe the bare bones of the evidence with comment and ideas on its meaning. This interpretation must be kept separate from the 'facts', even if these are by the nature of the excavation highly subjective, so that the latter are not obscured by the excavator's theories, and can if necessary be reinterpreted in the light of later knowledge; opinions may prove untrue, but facts remain. The excavator's reputation will not suffer if his interpretations prove incorrect, so long as the facts are accurate and consistent; sections must agree with plans, and the text with both; if there are discrepancies the whole report becomes suspect.

The facts and their interpretation are closely allied to the study of comparative material in other reports; it is by the integration of the new facts from the excavation with those already known that archaeological knowledge advances. Care must be taken to use the comparative evidence intelligently, and to quote it accurately. For example it is futile to quote a dating for a pot from another report unless it is fully understood on what basis the pot has there been dated.

A good report depends on a good recording system

The selection of material to be illustrated, the techniques of drawing the line figures, and the principles and standards involved in writing the report, have been discussed in the preceding pages. But exactly how is the report written? Many readers of the first printed edition of this book who were trying to write their first reports hoped that it would tell them how to proceed, rather in the manner of 'how to write a business letter'. Indeed in the opinion of one of our reviewers, Brian Hope-Taylor, it reduced the status of writing reports to just that level! Our readers found, however, that this was not what the book was about; it told them all about what the report should contain, but not how to write it.

Firstly, it must be emphasized that the planning of the report begins before the excavation starts. The standard of the report depends on how the evidence is obtained and recorded. No good report can be written on a dig that is carried out without method, whether of removing soil or of writing down or drawing the evidence. The excavator should be considering the final form of the report throughout the period of digging: he may well shape whole paragraphs in his mind as the evidence accrues and hypotheses develop.

The key to clear thinking and interpretation lies in the recording system used; this should be so designed that, among other things, all finds are directly related to some layer or feature which is described in the final report, either in text, section, plan, or photograph. Normally, the recording system will include some numbers and letters for layers, features, finds, etc. Correlation tables must be prepared to deposit with the finds, to show how the provenance marked on the objects relates to that in the published report.

If the excavation has been brought to a successful and unhurried conclusion it is to be hoped that the excavator will have formulated a 'story' which forms the basis of a short interim report or duplicated hand-out, written soon after the dig is finished. Matters such as periodization and the position of features, layers and finds within the general chronological sequence, should have been worked out while the dig was in progress (unless the 'rescue' nature of this has made it into a fast data-collecting operation). It only remains therefore for the hypothesis formulated to be checked in detail using all the available recorded evidence. Some find this easiest to do as soon after the dig as possible, while the whole subject is fresh in their minds, so that omissions in recording may be made good from memory aided by photographs. Others prefer to leave the report alone for some months so that when the report-writing begins it is done in a cool, retrospective state of mind, when a fresh and open approach may be brought to bear on the evidence.

If the dig was hasty, or the archaeological director inexperienced, or too many workers were involved at various levels of delegation, it may be that the major hypotheses concerning the structural and stratigraphical sequence on the site have not been fully worked out at the close of the excavation. In such cases, obviously nothing can be done in the way of writing a report until the basic material has been brought to order. 'How to write an archaeological report' is essentially how to arrange all the conclusions into an orderly form suitable for publication, not how to study the drawings, field notes, and finds and draw conclusions from them. Advice on how to do this is difficult to give, and is on the whole beyond the scope of this book: indeed it is a subject for a separate book, and may be an impossible thing to learn except by painful experience.

Nevertheless a few hints may be helpful, even to those who feel that they do know broadly what the excavation amounted to. The field drawings should be carefully studied, and preferably neatly traced off. Notes should be made of observations which can be deduced from these, and from a comparison of one with the other and with photographs, assuming that there are site records of the characteristics and finds associated with each feature and layer. These last should be edited and preferably typed on to index cards, making sure that all observations recorded on them are wholly consistent with all drawings and photographs.

The finds should next be studied, and information sought on them, as to their date, function, etc. This should lead to some conclusions about the dating and interpretation of features and layers. In particular, pottery evidence will be vital in establishing relationships between features and layers, in deciding which belong to the same period of occupation, and what layers are associated with building phases, etc.

Drawings of the finds may now be made, either by the excavator or by someone else if they are too difficult. All finds should be listed and described on index cards under each find class heading (see p. 66). If any are sent away for drawing or specialist examination, care must be taken to ensure that all obvious information has been extracted from them first, i.e. sketches, measurements, photographs, descriptions; these may be the only record if the finds are subsequently lost in transit or in a museum store. The more finds the archaeologist can draw himself the better he will understand them; this is especially true of pottery, which one really looks at or remembers only when it has been drawn by oneself. Reduced copies of drawings and photographs of finds should be pasted on to each find index card, so that it is as complete a record of the find as is possible at this stage.

Statistical lists will also be made now if not already done and material discarded where possible (see below, p. 66).

Much new information may eventually be received from outside specialists but the writing of the report should not be delayed until this has all been collected. There will usually be enough data available to enable a full report to be written, on to which new data can be grafted. It is not often that specialist reports will necessitate a complete recasting of the main report.

The object of all this preliminary sorting and tidying up is to enable the whole material on which the report is to be based to be spread out on a table. The finds will be stacked away somewhere and need only be referred to again in cases of difficulty. Muddy and torn field drawings will have been replaced by neat ones and can be put away. A set of annotated photographs can be available in loose sheets or in an album.

The material can now be studied and notes made on likely associations and explanations, including annotations on the drawings themselves. After all this preliminary work, some hypothesis should arise in the excavator's mind and can be checked by going through the material in detail. It is at this point that many beginners lose heart, and admittedly this is the most difficult part of writing a report. The experienced worker will have reached this stage before the excavation is finished when hypotheses can be checked on the ground.

After some time and study preferably uninterrupted over a period of days or weeks, the potential writer should be soaked in the material and can begin to compose a draft on the lines laid down in this book. A first draft should be written straight through from beginning to end, and typed. A typed version gives an air of (spurious) authority to any script and gives the writer confidence in his ultimate ability to produce a good report; this first typed complete draft is therefore a rock on which he can build.

On the basis of this draft the neat drawings can be annotated and prepared for their final version, incorporating all the conclusions that the writer has included in the first draft.

If the writer is experienced or feels confident that he understands the site without having written a first draft, he may decide to make all final drawings first. The text then becomes a commentary on the illustrations, and is easier for the reader to follow. If a first draft has been written, it may subsequently be rearranged to be such a commentary.

Preparation of the illustrations (see also Chapter 3)

It is convenient to prepare the drawings in their final form, and then have reduced copies made (about 203 mm. × 152 mm. for quarto, and 152 mm. × 101 mm. for octavo publications); these will incidentally show the extent to which the illustrations *can* be reduced without loss of detail. The finds should all be dealt with first, the drawings mounted in their final form, and reduced copies made. Thus all the finds and field drawings can be packed away before the text is begun; the whole evidence can then be put into a box-file or spread out conveniently on a table.

The illustrations have already been considered. It need only be repeated that they must be consistent, and they should show as much of the evidence as possible, in order that the text can be reduced to a minimum. It is possible that in the future reports will consist very largely of plans, sections, diagrams such as graphs, etc., linked only by the barest commentary, and referenced to detailed and extensive reports by specialists. (It should be noted however that one of the reviewers of our first printed edition, Martin Biddle, considered that such an end product was to be avoided since it dehumanized the whole subject). The plans and sections should proceed from the general to the particular. The following sequence may be found useful as a basis for writing the text:

1. Composite location map (see Chapter 3 and Fig. 1);
2. Plan of the site (see Chapter 3 and Fig. 2);
3. Detailed plans and sections of parts of excavations and features (see Chapter 3 and Fig. 4);
4. Interpretative drawings (see Chapter 3 and Figs. 5, 6);
5. Finds, in order of mineral, vegetable, and animal (see below and Figs. 7–12);
6. Illustrations to accompany specialist reports.

The plates will often be bound together at the end of the report, or sometimes at the end of the publication, well away from the report; it will be found convenient to paste on a board or card index copies of all photographs which may be published (although some may later be rejected by the editor on grounds of cost). They can then be referred to when the feature they illustrate is described in the text.

Arrangement of the text

The text can be shortened if the report is well illustrated. When the photographic copies have been spread out for reference it is wise to write down the framework of the report, the order of which should be logical and correspond with that of the illustrations. A typical sequence follows (note that specialist detail will be summarized in the text, and the reader referred to appendices):

1. Summary, introduction, and acknowledgments (see Chapter 2).
2. Description of the site:
    solid and drift geology;
    the subsoil encountered in the excavation and its relationship to the geology; the soils developed on the site;
    other environmental evidence, such as that of molluscs, fauna, flora, and climate; available materials, such as stone, coal, and water;
    food supplies: available game, fowl, fish, edible molluscs, etc.

The purpose of this section is to describe the whole environment which could have attracted settlers or builders to the site; this may explain why people *were* there in a particular period, or may draw attention to the poverty or hostility of the environment, in which case other factors (such as political ones or population pressure) may have to be invoked to explain human settlement.

3. The documentary evidence (mostly for post-Roman sites): this will describe in detail what was known about the site, its environs, or its occupants before excavation began. This may have to be a separate section contributed by a historian.

4. Previous references to earlier fieldwork or excavation.

5. The reasons for the present operation (these should justify destroying the site by excavation). The present state of the site (destroyed, flooded, pasture, etc.).

6. Extent of excavation, with reasons: labour force, finance, weather; methods adopted, with reasons (bulldozer or trowel, open or trench excavation); details of method or special equipment, if likely to be useful to other excavators on similar sites. This section is necessary to enable critical readers to judge the validity of the results, e.g. if a medieval peasant house were trenched it would explain to the reader why 'no walls were found'.

7. General description of results. This is more detailed than the summary, and should give a concise but complete picture of what has been found, but without, at this stage, full backing for the statements made. This may be in essay form, as in the excellent introductory pages to Wheeler (1943). It is often the only part of the report which is read by many readers.

8. Summary of main phases of occupation and the principal structures related to each. This will be more schematic than 7, and is really a 'contents list' for the detailed descriptions which follow and an indication of the nomenclature which is to be used

   e.g.: Phase I (Early Pre-Roman Iron Age): scatter of pottery and Pit 1.
   Phase II (a) (early Roman): timber house A: Pit 2; (b) (early Roman): rebuilding of house A.
   Phase III (late Roman): Stone house B.
   Phase IV (post Roman): (a) medieval lime-burning; (b) seventeenth century shepherd's hut.

   This summary may include the principal datable finds and mention key evidence.

9. Details of stratification: these will demonstrate the sequence of layers (or lack of them) on which the evidence is based. It may be necessary in a large report to codify the stratification recorded in different ways in different areas into a series of *master layers* numbered or lettered in the reverse order to that in which they were recorded in the field, i.e., from the bottom up. These may conveniently be prefixed M to distinguish them from ordinary layers, e.g. MA, MB, MC, etc.

10. Detailed description of each phase or structure: this is the *core* of the report, the evidence which is adduced to support the statements made in 7.
    Details should include:

(a) Dimensions of structures (although this information can be found on plans and/or sections, this will save the enquiring reader much time spent in scaling off measurements from those).

(b) Character and materials (how a feature is made, what it is made of).

(c) Details of individual stratification of pits, postholes, etc. – sometimes in tabular form.

(d) Dating evidence (referring forward to details of finds or specialist reports).

(e) The illustrations which show each feature or area described.

Some interpretation is inevitable in these descriptions. For example, a wall can safely be referred to as a 'wall', rather than as a 'regular arrangement of carefully shaped stones in line and in several layers', but words like 'timber-slots', 'cess-pit', or 'house' are more subjective, and should be used only if the evidence for their nature is stated.

11. Interpretation of remains found. This is the subjective part of the report which must be kept separate from the facts (especially by beginners; with experience they can be juxtaposed without confusion to help the reader). Reconstructions of the site should not be included if they are merely fanciful. The evidence for each should be carefully detailed and alternatives suggested to leave the reader with an open mind (compare the different reconstructions suggested for the farmhouse at Little Woodbury by Bersu (1940), Figs. 25, 26); the only exception to this is where it seems worthwhile to appeal to imagination in order to stimulate public interest, as with the excellent reconstructions of archaeological sites by Sorrell (1965).

12. Discussion. This can take many forms. Its purpose is to link the results described in the report to those from other sites, so that the subject of the report is considered in the light of contemporary research. Experienced writers will use this section as a means of formulating theories or suggesting further lines of research.

There is an unfortunate tendency for reviewers of reports to criticize this section rather than the factual body of the report. This may make the latter seem unreliable. Perhaps it would be better to keep all interpretation and discussion in separate publications, so that they can be considered independently of the data-collections comprised by the report?

Descriptions of Finds

These will normally be separate from the body of the report, so that the latter can be freed from detail which would side-track the reader's attention. Many editors have them set in small type to save space. They are, nevertheless, a vital part of the report, containing the evidence on which much or all of the interpretation is based.

There should be no distinction between 'descriptions of finds' and 'specialists' reports', although this distinction is sometimes and perhaps unwisely made. For instance, painted plaster is a find, but also a subject for scientific research into technique, and chemicals of pigments. Slags, though not always regarded as finds, are as important to the history of a site as brooches or coins.

Finds are only a means to an end, and are not, as often popularly supposed, the end-product of an excavation. Museums are partly the cause of this misconception, by presenting archaeology to the public as a series of finds in glass cases, without any hint of their use as archaeological data. The interest of all finds lies in the information they can provide on the whole history of the settlement or other site being excavated. To assess this information, the writer will have to consider for each find its (a) function, (b) dating, (c) technique of manufacture, (d) significance in art-historical studies; and they should be described in the report accordingly.

Selection of finds for illustration and description depends on how they have been recorded in the field; if a suitable system has been developed, much repetitive material, such as stone and pottery, can be discarded on the excavation (not elsewhere). A useful way of recording larger quantities of pottery is by creating a tentative *type-fabric series*, and possibly a *type-form series* as well, to which all pottery found is related, only significant pieces being retained for detailed description and illustration or for museum use.

The serial numbering of finds in the report depends on how many there are, and on editorial policy. It simplifies reference if all finds have a separate serial number, illustrated or not, running in sequence throughout the finds section; but this is far from being general practice.

The finds should be arranged in the order of their natural derivation – mineral, vegetable, and animal. This sequence has been adopted by the Laboratory of the Directorate of Ancient Monuments in the Department of the Environment to ensure objective assessment of each class of find, irrespective of its apparent importance, and to assist in achieving standardization of procedure. It must be pointed out, however, that this system has not yet been universally adopted. Exceptions will of course be made in the case of associated finds, such as grave-groups or well-deposits, which should be described as separate groups, though each of the components of the group may be described in its appropriate section as well.

(a) MINERAL

Stones (building materials, querns, hones, and other objects of stone; flint implements).

Coal, lignite, shale, jet.

Soils, developed from the basic geology.

Burnt clay (daub, oven remains, sling-bullets, loom-weights).

Fired clay, such as tiles, brick, and furnace-linings.

Pottery.

Mortar, stucco, plaster.

Glass.

Iron.

Copper alloys (bronze, etc.).

Other metals and alloys (gold, silver, tin, pewter, lead, etc.).

Slags.

(b) VEGETABLE

Wood (preserved as objects) or impressions of wood on metal objects.

Charcoal.

Other botanical material (including seeds, pips, and pollen).

Fibres and textiles (including cotton and rope), or their impressions on corroded metal objects or in clay, or their replacement by carbonate of lime.

(c) ANIMAL

Animal bones, and bone objects.

Molluscs (marine and freshwater).

Leather, fur, and wool.

Human bones.

Descriptions of finds should follow a consistent order which should include as many of the following details as are applicable:

(a) Material of which it is made. Spectrographic and other analyses can often assist.

(b) Function, if known; if not, the fact must be stated.

(c) Form: size and shape.

(d) Technique of manufacture: this should not be guessed. In some instances it will form the subject of a specialist report.

(e) Decoration.

(f) Method of use.

(g) *Internal* dating and context: what dating can be assigned to the object at *this* site, from its context.

(h) *External* dating and parallels: comparison with similar objects from other sites, and how they were dated there.

Large numbers of finds of the same kind may be described in groups, or tabulated, for the sake of brevity.

EXAMPLE

Iron; barrel padlock key; straight-shanked with spatulate bifurcated end; handle riveted to shank, which is hammered to square section; there are small incised chevrons on the shank below the handle; X-ray shows traces of non-ferrous metal plating; it was inserted into a barrel padlock of Smith's type B^i, the bifurcated end engaging in two pinions; it was found in layer G1, laid down as a make-up for a floor of *c*. A.D. 1550. A similar example found at Bigwood was there dated to the later sixteenth century.

POTTERY is a special case. Its treatment depends on the period (a single prehistoric sherd may be allocated a page or more) and how much is known already of that type of pottery in the area. The guiding principle in deciding what pottery to publish (especially out of large quantities of Roman or later pottery) is that it should be divided into three categories: (a) that which is being used as evidence for the dating or function of buildings or areas; (b) that which can be

67

assigned a dating or function because of the contexts in which it is found on the site; (c) that which is of intrinsic interest irrespective of context; this may well include most prehistoric or post-Roman/Saxon pottery.

Research would be facilitated if there were some standardized method of nomenclature and description, and a selection from the following headings is recommended:

(a) Whether a whole pot or part(s) of one are under consideration; if the latter, which parts and how much of each, e.g. part of the rim; all the base; half the spout.

(b) Form: jar, jug, bowl, or other vessel.

(c) Fabric: type of clay; grits; method of firing; colour and texture.

(d) Technique: whether wheel-turned or hand-made, and how finished.

(e) Glaze: apparent colour; texture; composition; how applied. A scientific report is required if possible.

(f) Decoration: appearance; technique; where applied.

(g) Internal context and dating.

(h) External parallels and dating.

EXAMPLE

No. 6. Half of rim, with edge of spout; bridge-spouted jug; brown soapy with some chalk grit; hand-made, finished on a turntable; edge of spout knife-trimmed; glossy patchy green-yellow lead-glaze, with traces of copper brushed on as powder (ref. to specialist's report); side of rim decorated with dot-and-circle, applied with a wooden stamp; jugs of this type were common in the later thirteenth century levels at Kidwelly (ref ....); found in the base of pit 12 (p. 345) with a coin of *c.* A.D. 1260 (p. 678).

Much of the information in a pottery description of this kind could, with a suitable system of coding be included in the drawing; an example of such a coding is given in Smith (1970).

Association of finds must be stressed. Large groups of pottery found together should be illustrated and described together, to show what kinds of pottery may be in use together; finds in the same context as a datable find such as a coin are themselves tentatively dated by this association. A convenient way of showing associations is by cross-referencing the finds, or by the use of tables: these can also be used to show unwieldy details clearly and concisely, but they can be expensive to print.

EXAMPLE

DITCH

NO.	AREA	PROFILE	FILLING	DATING	FINDS
7	J	V-shaped, flat base	Dark clayey silt	Period IIB, A.D. 80–100	Pottery (Fig. 16, nos. 1–10); Samian 6, 7 (A.D. 80–100), p. 64. Iron brooch (Fig. 8, no. 6). Quern no. 18 (p. 43).

Specialist reports

These may be contributed by scientists, art historians, documentary historians, philologists, or archaeologists. The increasing range and complexity of archaeological research have made it no longer possible for one man to be familiar with all aspects of the report he is writing. The archaeologist is increasingly dependent on specialists; but archaeologist and specialist are interdependent in that each gains information from the other. An excavation can provide specimens of material buried for a long time, which will help the specialist in his own research.

It is increasingly desirable that specialists should be involved in the collection of their own material, such as soil samples, pollen, and human bones. Not only can they get more information by observing the material *in situ*; but by being involved in the archaeology they are more likely to contribute information that is meaningful in the archaeological or historical context.

The arrangement of finds in the order mineral, vegetable, and animal, here recommended, is not the only possible arrangement. There is, for instance, much to be said in favour of arranging the finds by their function where this is either certain or probable. It is, for instance, illogical to separate objects connected with weaving into mineral (e.g. stone spindle-whorls), vegetable (e.g. wooden frames), and animal (e.g. bone weaving combs), and to describe them in different places in the report. British excavation reports have been adversely criticized on the ground that the mineral/vegetable/animal arrangement of the finds causes inadequate attention to be paid to their function.

Examples of excavation reports which classify the finds according to their function include Robinson (1941), Davidson (1952), and Warren (1972).

Too often the specialist has little idea of what the archaeologist is trying to find out: he receives and reports on the material in a vacuum. The result is often that his report is either unnecessarily long or obscure and seems to contribute little to the understanding of the site. The archaeologist (or editor) is then in the embarrassing position of having to ask him to shorten or clarify the report, a job which must *never* be done by the writer or the editor.

The full understanding of the scientific aspects of a site can often only be understood by integration of the various scientific reports. Often what one scientist reports is of direct relevance to the findings of another. There ought ideally to be some sort of scientific middleman or editor who is in full communication with all the scientists involved, who knows what questions should be asked of them, how to frame those questions, how to interpret the reports that are received, and correlate them in the final report. Few archaeologists are in a position to do this kind of liaison work (for a fuller discussion of this problem see Biek (1963)).

To summarize, it is useless to add specialist reports at the end of the text as appendices unless they say something worth saying, their meaning is fully understood, and the significant information incorporated in the text. It is important that any necessary amendments be made in the general report to bring it into line with the evidence from the specialist reports. When the proofs are received, the relevant section should be sent to each specialist, who should in due course receive an offprint of the whole publication. If the specialist contribution forms a major part of the report, his name should be included in the title, thus:

'The Roman Kiln at Renhill', by John Smith, with a report on the Pottery by Adrian Jones.

Treatment of folklore

It often happens that during an archaeological excavation local people visiting the site may disclose local beliefs, by asking whether the golden coffin, or golden calf, has yet been found, or is being searched for. Traditions of buried treasure are however only one of a wide range of types of folklore which can be associated with archaeological sites, and which were listed by Grinsell (1939). It is important that such traditions be placed on record somewhere. If the excavation report is destined for a local or county periodical the inclusion of folklore is likely to be acceptable to most editors. If it is intended for a national periodical the folklore might not fit in so well, and it can always be sent to the Editor, *Folklore*, c/o University College, Gower Street, London WC1E 6BT.

Interim reports

Excavations that are extended over more than one season are often the subject of interim reports, which should fulfil the following functions:

1. To convey information speedily and in summary form on the main results and chief finds of the previous season's work, so that it will be available to scholars and the public before the final report is published or perhaps even written.

2. To act as a fund-raiser by being distributed to subscribers to the season covered by the report, and to encourage these and others to subscribe to the forthcoming seasons of excavation. In the case of a big excavation such as Maiden Castle or South Cadbury, thousands of copies of these interim reports were sold at a considerable profit.

3. To provide a summary of the season's work for each of the volunteers in appreciation of their work, and as an encouragement for them to take part in the work of the following seasons.

4. In some instances (e.g. South Cadbury), interim reports of a special type were circulated to experts in Museums, University Departments, and elsewhere inviting their comments on the special problems raised by the excavation so far.

With these purposes in mind it will be evident that the interim report should be written in a manner calculated to stimulate enthusiasm among its readers, even to the extent of causing them to bring out their cheque books. A dry-as-dust approach, involving tedious descriptions of sections and unimportant finds, should be avoided. The reader must be convinced that his last donation was well spent and that his future donations will be used to solve outstanding problems which should be clearly specified, and which are really worth solving. It is good policy to get a publicity official to read and comment on the interim report from this standpoint; any recommendations that he may make should be considered and perhaps adopted before the report is finalized and distributed.

All information of permanent value in these interim reports should be carried forward to the final report, which should in fact supersede them. It should be made clear that any conclusions expressed in interim reports are provisional and subject to modification or even reversal if subsequent excavations produce new and different evidence. In these days of high printing costs it is not essential for interim reports to be printed to such a high standard as the final report, and even duplicating or multigraphing is permissible, but some form of photo-printing is preferable as it tends to give a better impression to prospective donors.

Finally, publication of interim reports must *never* be used as an excuse for not producing a final report.

5

THE BODY OF A NON-EXCAVATIONAL REPORT

Leslie Grinsell

> Rare birds, these, of which it would be nice to see more.
> MARGARET GELLING, Review of the first (printed) edition of *The Preparation of Archaeological Reports*, in *Trans. Birmingham Archaeol. Soc.* LXXXII for 1965, (1967), 100

(Much of the information in this chapter may be useful also to those preparing excavation reports.)

This type of report has one great advantage over the excavation report: normally it contains no specialist appendices or contributions and therefore it is under the sole control of the author who has only himself to blame if he does not complete it by whatever deadline has been set by his editor or himself. If such a report does include specialist contributions they tend to be of the type which is not dependent on examination or analysis of artifacts, and to be of the order of geological or geographical appraisals; comments on Anglo-Saxon land charters or other documentary sources; or contributions on place names, local names, or field names. These can usually be written without the sort of delay that is notoriously associated with excavators' specialist reports.

Non-excavational reports deal usually with either field archaeology or small finds, or both. Inevitably they make use of material derived from excavations as well as field observations and the study of material in museums and private collections. They range over a wide variety of subjects the scope of which is indicated in Appendix B. In many instances they deal with one parish or small area only, when they may cover every period from palaeolithic to post-medieval or industrial. A type of non-excavational report which has been popular for many years is the area survey on a county, regional, national, or international basis, usually limited to the study of one period only. The following suggestions are made with this type of report in mind, but to a limited extent they should be useful in preparing other kinds of report.

The most important form of preparation for writing *any* report of this type is the careful study of other reports on the same subject or related subjects. Those listed in Appendix B cover many aspects and periods, but a search through the national and regional periodicals will reveal many other good examples. The reports listed in that Appendix are confined to the British Isles, but fresh ideas can be obtained by searching recent volumes of the various foreign archaeological periodicals. Among these may be mentioned *Palaeohistoria* (Groningen) and *Förnvannen* (Stockholm) both of which contain articles in English or with English summaries.

An analysis of the longer reports listed in Appendix B, and others, shows that most of them have the following structure:

    Summary.
    Introduction.
       History of study?
       Acknowledgments.
  I. Classification.
 II. Relative chronology and dating.
III. Structure (field monuments).
    Composition and method of manufacture (implements).
    Decoration (where applicable, e.g. rock-carvings; various types of implement and ornament).
 IV. The native and foreign elements.
  V. Distribution (include Maps).
 VI. Conclusion (should indicate future needs).
    References and Bibliography.
    Inventory of material studied.

Most reports will have a slant which may require modification of this framework, e.g. by adapting section III to the subject at hand, or by adding sections on geology of sources of the raw materials of which the field monuments or small artifacts are composed. The writer's own reports on regional surveys of barrows, for instance, include sections on their local names and folklore, and their later history.

If a report is long enough to be divided into Parts I, II, III and so on, it is as well to follow the number with a statement of the subject, thus: I. Classification and Nomenclature. There is no reason why the reader should have to read through a whole section to find out what it is about. It is well to consider these sections in detail.

The summary

If the paper is more than about twenty pages long, it will be useful to precede it by a summary on the lines set forth in Chapter 2.

Introduction

The writer will usually wish to explain the circumstances which led to the study. It might be adapted from a University thesis, or it might have resulted from an interest developed as the result of a local find. As a rule this is a fairly easy paragraph to produce in first draft and it will probably be improved later on. Acknowledgments of assistance received can also fit well into this or a following paragraph under this heading. If they are many they can be given a separate heading.

The present writer would like to see more papers devoting at least a paragraph, possibly in this introduction, to a brief outline of previous work done on the subject. There are too many people who plunge into a paper without mastering what has already been written on their subject. A survey of all previous relevant literature is surely an essential qualification for a fresh study. The practice of some archaeologists to disparage the work of their predecessors should here be avoided, but their general shortcomings (by modern standards) should none the less be mentioned. Their errors in matters of detail are best noted in the Inventory.

I. Classification

Providing that the writer has acquired a mastery of his material and studied all available sources in the field, the museum and the library, the writing of this section should present no difficulties that he cannot easily solve. It might however be worth mentioning that several archaeologists (including the author) now admit to having tended to over-classify in their earlier studies (Grinsell, 1934).

II. Relative chronology and dating

This section cannot be written until the inventory has been completed and all sites (or small objects) which can be dated by association given special attention. It is among the most important sections in the paper and is likely to be the most difficult one to write. The relative chronology is usually not too difficult to establish, but the absolute dating (if prehistoric) may involve weighing the merits of radiocarbon dating with bristlecone pine correction, in the light of the knowledge of the moment. It is now becoming standard practice to use 'b.c.' for uncorrected radiocarbon dates and 'B.C.' for radiocarbon dates corrected by bristlecone pine calibration; but when this practice is followed the fact should be stated at the first mention.

III. Structure; composition; decoration

This section is likely to be the most variable of all in content according to the subject of the report. Here again it is a matter of studying the most authoritative (not necessarily the most recent) relevant reports and literature. Most (but not all) the best work on these aspects has been done since the 1939/45 War and will therefore usually appear in the post-war literature.

IV. **The native and foreign elements**

In this context it is essential to read Clark (1966) on 'The Invasion hypothesis in British Archaeology'. Between the two World Wars there was too great a tendency to 'derive' archaeological material from various foreign and especially Mediterranean influences, and the indigenous contribution tended to be neglected or underestimated. The subject has recently been reviewed for prehistory by G. E. Daniel (1971) and Renfrew (1973), and for all periods by Bowen (1972), 8–9 and *passim*.

V. **Distribution**

The preparation of distribution maps is the subject of the next chapter. Here it is necessary to say a little about their interpretation. In order to interpret an archaeological distribution map intelligently, it is necessary first of all to have an adequate knowledge of the geography and geology of the area which it covers. On the solid geology depends the scope for man's exploitation of economic resources including stone for building and for axe-heads, whetstones, querns and many other purposes, and metalliferous and non-metalliferous sources of useful raw materials. On the drift geology, modified here and there by man's own activities, depends the distribution of human settlement. Whatever period is the subject of one's own study, it is a great advantage to have a working knowledge of the history of the area from palaeolithic times until the present day, to get an idea of the settlement pattern in each period at any rate in broad outline. This will provide a context within which to study the distribution map of the period under consideration.

The limitations in the inventory on which the distribution-pattern is based have now to be considered. If the inventory is of field monuments, how many have been destroyed by cultivation, economic development, and other human activity in later periods? To what extent do aerial photographs indicate how much has been destroyed? One has only to see the aerial photographs of the large numbers of sites in the Middle and Upper Thames valley and many other river valleys in other parts of Britain to understand how incomplete is the evidence represented by existing field monuments. If the inventory is of chance finds, to what extent is a map of palaeolithic implements, for example, related to the nineteenth century exploitation of brick-earth? Perhaps as much as 90 per cent and such a map may serve equally well, if not better, as a distribution map of the nineteenth century exploitation of brick-earth. To what extent is the distribution of hoards of Bronze Age bronze implements along the south coast due to the development of much of the coastal strip for holiday resorts?

It has recently been written that 'by the production of accurate land-use maps for the post-Roman periods, we can see how much of what we find of prehistoric and Roman date is related to the inevitable destruction of later centuries and how many of our ideas on the distribution and density of settlement, as well as estimates of population, need revision' (Taylor, 1972). It is therefore necessary to have later land-use constantly in mind when interpreting all archaeological distributions.

In general, some of the most reliable interpretations of archaeological distributions have been made by archaeologists originally trained as geographers, e.g. O. G. S. Crawford, D. J. Bonney, H. J. Fleure, E. G. Bowen, and Bruce Proudfoot. It is just as well to discuss one's own interpretations with a geographer before finalizing them.

VI. Conclusion

This section normally presents no difficulties if it is written after the rest of the report has been completed. Some writers will put this in the form of 'Summary and Conclusions', in which case it would either replace, or be a little more expansive and detailed, than the summary given at the start of the report. In some instances it might well take the form of a commentary on the sum of the evidence presented statistically in the form of one or more tables or diagrams. It should include an indication of aspects where further investigation is desirable, and relevant problems outstanding.

References and bibliography (see Chapter 7)

Inventory of material studied

The best published inventories of comparable material should be consulted in preparation for compiling this most important section. Measurements should henceforth be given metric. Topographical location of find-spots should be given on the National Grid reference system, to as many eastings and northings as the evidence will allow. With regard to County and Parish, it has of course been until now the custom to give these wherever possible, but the revision of local government boundaries, affecting several county boundaries, will present a serious problem. Those people are fortunate whose county is unaffected by the change. The best advice that can be given at the moment is to state at the top of the Inventory whether it is arranged under the traditional or the new boundaries so that the reader knows where he stands.

The inventory should include an indication of which museum or collection houses the object or the material from the excavation of each site. Whether references to publications should be included in the inventory depends on the context. Ideally the answer should be 'yes', but there are certain types of report where this may not be practicable, for instance in a report on the petrological identification of 1200 stone implements (Evens and others, 1962).

6

DISTRIBUTION MAPS

Leslie Grinsell

> The time aspect demands a chronological system,
> and the space aspect a series of distribution maps.
> O. G. S. CRAWFORD, *Archaeology in the Field* (1953), 40

It is recommended that base-map and overlays (distribution patterns) be produced separately, at least in the first instance. Almost any well-drawn base-map is likely to be used more than once and many are likely to be used for dozens of different distribution overlays. It is worth while trying to persuade an editor to sanction the inclusion of two-colour distribution maps. Failing this, it is possible to produce a two-tone distribution map in only one colour by producing the base-map with Letraset or other dry-transfer appliances, by using one of their forms of mechanical stippling, and then using fairly heavy symbols for the overlay (Coles, 1963, Fig. 13). A similar result can of course be achieved by drawing the base-map by hand with fine stippling or discontinuous lines to produce a grey effect. It is worth trying publishers of outline maps, such as W. & A. K. Johnston Ltd., or G. Philip & Son Ltd., who sometimes produce excellent outline maps which can be used either as they are, or as a basis for one which meets the archaeologist's requirements more precisely.

Drawings for both base-maps and distribution overlays should always be made on plastic sheet such as Permatrace or Ozalid, as they are dimensionally stable under all normal changes of temperature or humidity. This dimensional stability is essential to ensure correct registration of the overlays on the base-map if they are drawn on separate sheets or to be printed from separate blocks.

The base-map

This should always be drawn before preparing the distribution overlays. It should be prepared from an Ordnance Survey map which is National-Gridded,

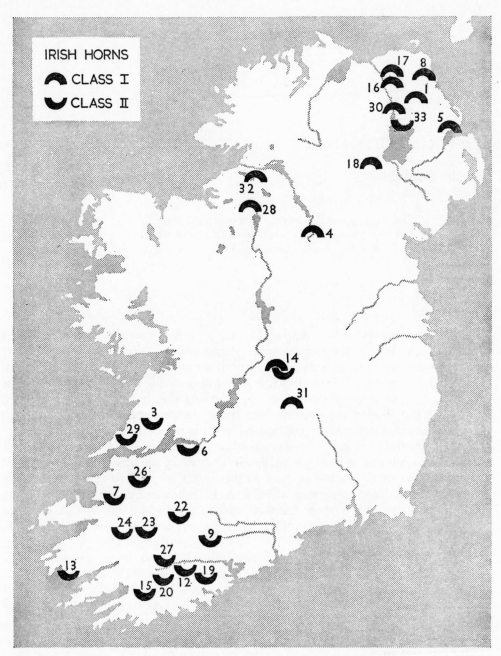

Fig. 13 Map showing two tones printed by one block. Distribution in Ireland of Bronze Age horns. J. M. Coles, *Proc. Prehist. Soc.* XXIX, 1963, 331

as this will greatly facilitate the plotting of the locations on the overlays. It should be drawn between twice and three times the linear dimensions of the map as intended for publication. First of all, the National Grid squares of the area to be covered should be indicated at any rate in pencil, and the area to be covered finalized. Then the coastline (if any) and political or other regional land boundaries should be drawn, preferably with a fairly thick line for the coastline and a dot-and-dash line for the land boundaries. The appearance of any map showing a coastline can be vastly improved by thoughtful treatment of the sea or the coast. The shoreline can be indicated by stippling (Fig. 16); by a series of two or more parallel lines getting thinner and wider apart as they increase in distance from the coast; by shading in horizontal parallel lines, or (perhaps best of all) by a horizontal ripple, which can easily be drawn freehand if controlled by the use of squared (graph) backing paper, or applied by a mechanical dry-transfer such as Letraset LT 118 (large ripples) or LT 126 (small ripples).

The addition of rivers and relief or geology (either solid or drift) will assist in interpreting the distribution pattern. For obvious reasons the adding of rivers must be highly selective, and in the first instance it is best to add only the most important rivers and any others known to have influenced human settlement. Others can be added as required by the development of the overlays. In drawing the rivers, it should be borne in mind that at a later stage the river names will have to be added; and a decision should be taken on whether they should be written above the rivers, or 'in' them by removing any of the straighter portions long enough to accommodate the name. With rivers flowing through narrow valleys the latter choice may well be preferable: the Exmoor rivers are a case in point (Grinsell, 1970). It is astonishing how many archaeological distribution maps are being published which show no rivers at all and thereby reduce their utility to a minimum and make interpretation of the overlays almost a farce.

For a base-map to be informative when the distribution overlays are superimposed, land detail of some kind should be shown. It may be hill-contoured without or with shading, or shaded to accord with the solid or drift geology. For normal purposes, base-maps showing hill-contours at two or three levels, preferably suitably shaded, are straightforward to prepare and effective in use (Grimes, 1963; Grinsell, 1970). The task of drawing a base-map showing either solid or drift geology tends to be more laborious and that is probably why most archaeologists go to press on layered (contour-shaded) base-maps. The extra effort in producing a geological base-map sometimes has its rewards. For Wessex, the spread of settlement from the chalk downland to the heaths during the Bronze Age is thereby clearly shown, as well as the rarity of round barrows on those parts of the chalk downland which are covered with clay-with-flints and other superficial deposits (Grinsell, 1941, 1958). Such maps also show the rarity of prehistoric settlement on the clays. A drift geology base-map would seem to be most suitable for period overlays of settlements based primarily on an agricultural or pastoral economy; and a solid geology base-map may be appropriate for mapping settlements based primarily on a mining and industrial economy. It might be possible to produce a compromise base-map when the settlement pattern resulted from a mixed economy.

It is desirable to include a reasonable number of place-names on the base-map, because if they are added to the distribution overlays they will spoil the pattern. Names of the major towns should therefore be added, and also any other place-names likely to be mentioned in the accompanying text.

It has for many years been a standard convention among government and most other professional cartographers, on both sides of the Iron Curtain, to use *italic* capitals for the names of seas and estuaries, and *italic* lower case for the names of rivers and streams and other smaller water surfaces including lakes. The *italic* fount has a 'liquid' appearance and can be easily fitted into the often sinuous courses of rivers. By contrast it is convenient to use Roman lettering for place-names. Names of tribes and tribal areas of the Iron Age (not quite so static) are, however, often shown in *italic* capitals.

When preparing a series of period distribution maps, the writer has found it essential to test each period overlay with the base-map by drawing the overlays on plastic sheet and superimposing each on the base-map. Assuming that the distribution maps are the result of physical fieldwork as distinct from 'travels in one's study', this process will involve the making of certain minor corrections to the base-map: the lengthening of a river here, or the adding of a small river not previously shown; the amendment of a contour there, or a slight change in the coastline somewhere else. Where a series of period overlays has been prepared, it will be found that a study of each in relation to the base-map will necessitate a few slight alterations in the latter, which cannot therefore be finalized until each overlay has been tested against it (Grinsell, 1958, 1965, 1970).

Finally, if the national grid square divisions are retained on the published map they should of course be lettered and numbered. It seems best to add North point and scale although these are often omitted in the case of general maps such as a map of England. There is no reason why the North point should not be made to look attractive providing that it is not so ornate as to draw attention away from the overlays. In the case of a series of period maps, the North point can with advantage be omitted from the base-map but added to the overlays and varied in design so as to be appropriate to the period of each overlay. Above all, the use of some of the extremely ugly dry-transfer North points now on the market should be avoided. For the next ten years or so it is desirable to give the scale in both kilometres and miles.

The distribution overlays

These should be prepared on plastic sheets superimposed on the base-map. The present writer always starts by inserting the four corners of the base-map to ensure exact registration between overlay and base-map.

Ceremonial Sites

Stone Circle

Earthen Circle

Stone Row

Stone Setting

Standing Stone

Temple (Iron Age or Roman)

Defensive Sites

Hill-fort, univallate

Hill-fort, multivallate

Cliff-castle
  (sited to promontory)

Rampart

Ditch

Living Sites

Inhabited Cave

Lake Village

Hill-slope Enclosure

Hill-slope Enclosure
  (with outworks)

Other Enclosure

Industrial Sites

Mine or Quarry

Kiln, for pottery

Kiln, for tiles

Communications

Road (Roman)

Trackway

Burial Sites

Long Barrow
  (correctly orientated)

Burial Chamber
  (shape of original
    mound uncertain)

Round Barrow: Bowl

             Bell

             Disc

Single Grave

War Grave

Cemetery

War Cemetery

Miscellaneous

Submerged Forest

Shipwreck (Roman)

Fig. 14   Some symbols recommended for field monuments. A wide range of additional symbols is given in the keys to the Ordnance Survey period maps, especially those on *Southern Britain in the Iron Age* and *Roman Britain*. There is a need for a commercially produced stencil for archaeological symbols most frequently used. In general principle, the writer considers that the most successful maps of distribution of small artefacts are produced by the use of a straightforward circle or other simple symbol, and the type of object mapped to be shown by a sketch in an otherwise unused corner of the map

The coastline (if any)

If, during the period represented by the period overlay, the coastline was different from that of today, the conjectured coastline of the period can be indicated on the overlay (Cunliffe, 1966).

The objects to be mapped

The type of object which is the subject of the distribution map can be illustrated by a drawing in an otherwise blank part of the map, as it is essential that the reader be left in no doubt as to what is being mapped (Piggott, 1938). In general there should be a separate map for each type of object; but sometimes two or three types can be effectively shown as contrasting or similar distribution patterns on the same base-map. Further multiplicity of types of object by the use of several different symbols on the same base-map usually results in confusion.

The shape and size of the symbols (Figs. 13–16)

(a) SHAPE. It has recently been written that 'the ideal symbol should be so designed that the reader immediately associates it with whatever feature it indicates without reference to a legend or key' (Hodgkiss, 1970, 109). In the opinion of the present writer, representational symbols are a failure if they are long and thin. Symbols as broad as they are long are generally the most effective, and these include circles, squares, equilateral triangles and equal-armed crosses, of which all can be varied in size for different types of site or find, and the first three can be either solid or open. A distinction between precisely and only vaguely known find-spots can be made by the use of large and small symbols or of solid and open symbols, care being given to give less weight to the vaguely known find-spots. Similarly, in the case of field monuments, a certain example can be shown by a solid, and a doubtful one by an open symbol. The principle of designing symbols in the form of miniature drawings of the objects represented is in the writer's opinion a failure if carried out on a large scale (Grinsell, 1957). It can however be successful with certain types of object such as gold lunulae (Fox, 1932) or bronze horns (Coles, 1963; Fig. 13). The use of letters as symbols is not very effective and can border on failure (Allen, 1961). The use of certain shapes of symbol for particular types of antiquity has for many years received general acceptance, e.g. circles (single or concentric, solid or open) for Iron Age hill-forts, and triangles for Roman villas. It is wise to follow such standard practice unless there are strong reasons for departing from it. The Ordnance Survey period maps provide excellent guidance on this.

In an illuminating report by Sir John Evans (1876), proposals for an international code of symbols for use on archaeological maps suggested the adoption of *radical* symbols (such as those described), and *derived* symbols, which adopt the radical symbol for the object, but provide extra information by adding to it. For example, an open circle can represent a round barrow and a solid circle can be used for one that has been excavated with known result (Philip Crocker followed

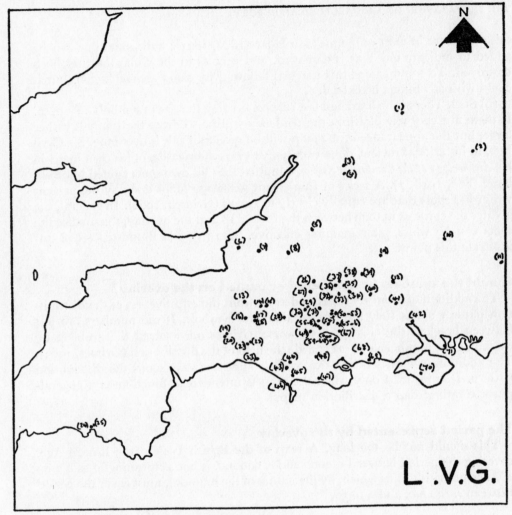

Fig. 15   How not to draw a distribution map
The Coins of the Durotriges. Based on R. P. Mack, *The Coinage of Ancient Britain*, 2nd edn
(1964), 116
1.   No proper distinction between land and sea
2.   No rivers
3.   North point too large and also ugly, and scarcely necessary on a general map of
this type
4.   Spots too small, drawn freehand, and lacking in uniformity
5.   Pattern spoiled by addition of site-numbers, made worse by being written freehand
and enclosed in brackets
6.   No distinction made between hoards and single finds
7.   Initials of cartographer are too large and badly spaced; in any case they should not
have been inserted because the distribution has been copied from the source stated
8.   Area covered by map does not include the whole of the known distribution; in
particular it omits the vitally important hoard from Jersey

this procedure in most of the maps in Hoare 1812, 1821); a diagonal line can be added to indicate one that is damaged, and a cross to show one that has been destroyed. To some extent this usage is followed by some archaeologists, but it could with advantage be extended.

(b) SIZE. There is no hard and fast rule concerning the size of symbols on a map. If there are very few plottings the tendency will be to draw the symbols rather large, but the appearance of the map will be spoiled if this is overdone. Sir Cyril Fox, in his critical review, done twenty-five years afterwards, of his own maps in his *Archaeology of the Cambridge Region*, admitted that his own spots tended to be too large (Fox, 1948, 7). A series of Implement petrology maps done by the present writer has spots that are equally clearly too small (Grinsell, 1962). In general, the greater the contrast in tone between the base-map and the overlay, the smaller the spots can be while yet remaining effective. The maps in Brøndsted (1938–40) illustrate this point.

Should the symbols be numbered or named on the overlay?

The addition of numbers tends to detract from the effectiveness of the distribution pattern unless they are smaller than the symbols. If the numbers are put between brackets the effect is even worse. Grimes once solved the problem by extending the numbers to areas outside the field of the distribution (Grimes, 1963). The addition of names beside the symbols almost always spoils the distribution pattern. It is justified only when the map is intended to function as a general-purpose rather than a distribution map.

The period represented by the overlay

This should not be too long. A map of the British Isles in the Bronze Age, covering the period between *c.* 2000 and *c.* 600 B.C. is not as meaningful as a map of Ancient British coins which, by the nature of the material, must cover the period between *c.* 100 B.C. and A.D. 50.

The area represented by the overlay

Sometimes it happens that although the base-map covers, for example, the whole of England or the British Isles, the data mapped have been assembled for only a part of the area. In such instances the area for which the data are comprehensive should be distinguished from the rest of the area of the base-map by a line of dots or dashes (Grinsell, 1962).

The mapping of negative evidence

Where, for example, several excavations of sites of a particular period in a region have failed to yield a specific type of pottery found elsewhere, the fact can be shown by the use of a special symbol, which should if possible have a 'negative' appearance (Jope, 1963).

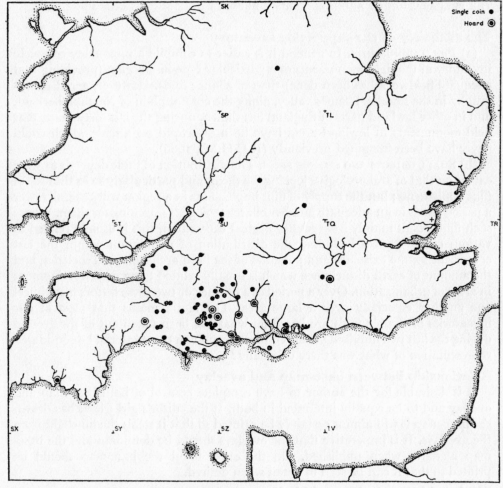

Fig. 16   How to draw a distribution map
The Coins of the Durotriges. Based on R. P. Mack, *The Coinage of Ancient Britain*, 2nd edn (1964), 116
1.   Coastline emphasised by stippling
2.   Main rivers shown
3.   North point omitted as Grid North implied by the lettered divisions
4.   Spots about the right size and traced by standardgraph stencil and therefore of uniform size. (Dry transfer by Letraset or similar method would have been equally effective)
5.   Numbers within brackets omitted in order not to confuse the distribution pattern. Angles and letter prefixes to national grid squares have been sited so as not to detract from the distribution pattern. Their purpose is to control plotting and to enable the reader to check the spots with any accompanying inventory
6.   A distinction has been made between hoards and single finds
7.   Initials of cartographer omitted as unnecessary
8.   Area of map extended to include the whole known distribution area, including the hoard of crucial importance from Grouville, Jersey

The adequacy of the supporting inventory

(a) FIELD MONUMENTS. In general it is easier to compile a reasonably complete inventory of the field monuments of a particular type in a region (providing that adequate fieldwork has been done) than of chance finds. However, aerial photography in the middle Thames valley, along the coastal plain of Northumberland, and in other lowland parts of England has shown, during the last forty years, that field monuments in lowland areas have been destroyed on a scale which could never have been imagined previously (R.C.H.M., 1960).

(b) SMALL OBJECTS AND CHANCE FINDS. The distribution of these depends to some extent on that of archaeologists looking for them, and particularly so in the case of flint implements; but the supply of flint implements in a region will generally over a period result in an adequate number of archaeologists searching for them. Where such finds result mainly from archaeological excavation, this is usually related to various circumstances including the distribution of population within the last century or so, the existence and potential of the local archaeological societies, and the amount of earth disturbance which is usually related to modern development in areas of urbanization. Over a period of a century or two these factors may cancel one another especially over a large area. The fact remains that most of our inventories of chance finds are based on what has been taken out of the ground during the last two hundred years. To what extent can that material be considered representative of what was there originally?

Relationship between base-map and overlay

It is desirable for the author to have complete control of both base-map and overlay and to be equally interested in both. If the editor's girl friend has drawn the base-map it will almost certainly be printed so that it steals the limelight from the overlays. It is imperative that the overlays should be dominant and the base-map recessive when published. On the other hand the base-map should be printed so that it can be seen in detail when desired.

Blockmaking, printing and binding

In his chapter 'How not to write local history', Finberg (1967, 78) has this to say on maps: 'let the blockmaker reduce it so drastically that most names become illegible; and finally let the binder insert it into the book in such a way that it tears every time you open it'. It is enough to add that all the trouble taken in drawing a perfect base-map with overlays can be thrown away by bad editing or bad printing or binding.

Copyright

If a base-map is drawn from an Ordnance Survey map published more than fifty years ago there is no copyright to be cleared; but the imposition of a national grid on such a map is enough to attract a copyright fee. Strictly speaking, any base-map drawn from or founded substantially on a more recent Ordnance Survey map needs copyright clearance. Any approach to the Ordnance Survey for this purpose is preferably made by the editor rather than the author (see p. 37).

7

THE FINAL STAGES

Leslie Grinsell

> This is the fynal ende of al this thyng
> CHAUCER, *The Legend of Good Women*. Ariadne, line 2101

Arrangement and contents list

In the case of major papers, it will be a great help to both editor and printer if the author places at the beginning of his paper an arrangement of headings and sub-headings corresponding to those given in the body of the paper, indicating their relative importance, somewhat in the following manner:

1. Capitals triple-underlined
2. Capitals double-underlined
3. Capitals single underlined
4. Capitals without underline
5. Lower case underlined (for printing in *italic*)
6. Lower case without underline.

This will assist the editor to decide, in consultation with the printer, on type faces to be used. The author should also indicate his own preference on which of these sub-headings should be centralized and which should start at the left margin. The ultimate decision on such matters rests with the editor who has to conform to the house style of his periodical, but it does no harm to acquaint him with the author's wishes.

Notes and references

Almost all reputable periodicals now follow the Harvard system of giving references in the following form:

In text: Clark (1954), 59. Some editors prefer the form Clark 1954, 59.

In references: Clark, J. G. D. (1954). *Excavations at Star Carr*. Cambridge.

Many editors prefer to have the initials of the author in the text, but this is not necessary unless the full list of references or bibliography gives more than one author of the same name, when, of course, they have to be distinguished. In the case of reprinted books, it is usual to follow the date of the reprint by that of the original publication, thus: (1974) (1953). The more recent date only need be quoted in the text.

Titles of periodicals should be abbreviated in a consistent manner. The list of abbreviations for current British archaeological periodicals, recommended by the Council for British Archaeology, is given on pp. 9–15, together with the present writer's comments. It seems best to follow the C.B.A. recommended abbreviations unless the periodical for which one is writing has its own system of abbreviations.

The volume number can be given in either Roman (e.g. III) or Arabic (e.g. 3) numerals according to the house style of the periodical. The Roman numerals can be in upper or lower case according to the house style, and the Arabic numerals can with advantage be set in bold face to differentiate them from the page numbers which will follow. In this text, Roman numerals are used to conform to the publisher's house style; but the present trend is in favour of using bold-face Arabic numerals as these are cheaper to set and easier to read, e.g. **78** and not LXXVIII.

We now come to a problem on which experts disagree. The Harvard system requires that the author's name be followed by the date of publication of his book (or paper). Most archaeological periodicals are issued on the basis of a volume for each year against an annual subscription; but many of these volumes are as much as two or three years in arrear. For example, Mrs M. Gelling's review of the 1966 edition of this book appeared in *Trans. Birmingham Archaeol. Soc.* LXXXII for 1965, published in 1967. The recommendation here made is to give the *date of publication* after the author's name, and to follow the volume number of the periodical with the year *for* which it was issued, within round brackets, *when that differs from the date of publication*. This should eliminate the risk of confusion, while keeping printing costs down to a practical minimum.

By way of illustration:

Roberts (1965). Roberts, B. K. (1965). 'Moats and Mottes', *Medieval Archaeol.* VIII (for 1964), 219–222.

Roe (1966). Roe, F. E. S. (1966). 'The Battle-Axe Series in Britain', *Proc. Prehist. Soc.* XXXII, 199–245.

In the latter instance the volume was issued in December 1966. It is as well to state at the top of one's list of references that this policy is being followed if such is the case.

In the printed version of the report, the titles of books and the titles of the publications of learned societies have to be set in italics; but the titles of papers in the Proceedings or Transactions of learned societies are set between inverted commas, usually single. If the titles of books and of the publications of learned societies are underlined in the typescript, the printer will understand that they are to be set in italics. It is wise to observe this rule even when the publication is to be duplicated or printed by photo-lithography.

Editorial alterations

It is probable that the editor will make a few amendments in the text before sending the paper to the printer. Editors vary from those who will never alter so much as a comma without consulting their author, to those who think nothing of re-writing or deleting whole paragraphs, with or without the consent of their author. Strictly speaking, an editor should not make alterations unless he is able to justify his actions to his author. Authors likewise range from those who raise no objection to normal editorial alterations, to those who take great offence at the slightest amendment made without their approval.

The need for sympathy and understanding between author and editor is therefore self-evident. It is the duty of a good editor to try to achieve the highest attainable standard among all his contributors, and also to ensure that they all conform, as far as possible, to the house style of his periodical.

It is important that editors make their amendments *before* sending the paper to the printers; the writer has known editors who have been badly at fault in this respect.

Correcting the proofs

Among the best small books on proof-correcting are the Oxford University Press *Rules for Compositors and Readers*, by H. Hart; and the Cambridge University Press pamphlet on *Preparation of Manuscripts and Correction of Proofs* by B. Crutchley. Most printers tend to follow the rules of one or other of these presses, which rather differ in detail. Another useful book is the *Authors' and Printers' Dictionary*, by F. Howard Collins (Oxford University Press). These books are also useful for looking up doubtful points in the course of one's writing. The pamphlet, *Authors' Alterations Cost Money and Cause Delay* (British Federation of Master Printers, 11 Bedford Row, London WC1) should be read by all concerned.

It is always desirable to mark author's corrections in ink of one colour, and printers' errors in ink of another colour. The British Federation of Master Printers has recently recommended that printers mark their own corrections in green, and authors and publishers mark theirs in blue or black, and indicate printers' errors in red. Printers usually indicate their own wishes on this subject when sending the proofs.

The galleys

The galleys of short reports are likely to be the only proofs which an author will see, and the greatest care must therefore be taken to ensure that no errors are overlooked. A colleague may well spot errors that an author has missed more than once. With longer reports, it is the proper course of a considerate editor to allow his author to see his work in page-proof. Care should still be taken to ensure that all corrections are made at galley stage, as *no alterations involving increases or decreases in the length of the text can be made in page-proof*, without involving the costly process of re-paging.

The page-proofs

An author receiving the page-proofs should check all the alterations made in galley to ensure that they have been correctly made by the printer. He can do this only if the printer returns the galleys with the page-proofs, or if the author has retained a spare set of the galleys with all the alterations made that were on the set which was returned to the printers. This task must be taken seriously as it is the author's last chance to spot any errors that remain.

It is also advisable to read the whole of the text through once again to make sure that no statements made have been invalidated or rendered doubtful by any knowledge recently acquired by the author. With a rapidly developing subject such as archaeology, an author who keeps abreast of his subject is almost bound to have one or two such alterations to make in a lengthy paper, and a considerate editor should be sensible about this. At this stage it is necessary to complete any cross-references between pages, and to ensure that references to illustrations have been made (this should be taken as far as possible in galley stage, but the page numbers can be inserted only when the work is in page-proof).

There should be some kind of gentlemen's agreement between author and editor that if the editor allows the author to see the page-proofs, the author will exercise proper restraint by avoiding unnecessary alterations. It is a good plan for an editor to allow an author a certain number of corrections free, but to charge him for corrections above that limit. *Both galleys and page-proofs should be corrected as soon as possible after they have been received, and returned to the editor without delay.*

There is an increasing tendency on the part of publishers and editors to put the author's copy straight into page-proof, thereby saving time and money. This growing practice underlines the importance of the author sending in his typescript word-perfect and in the state in which he desires it to be printed.

It is a breach of etiquette for an author to deal direct with the printer of an archaeological periodical unless its editor has expressly authorized him to do so.

The index

If the report is lengthy or to be published as a monograph it will require its own index. Very few archaeological publications are really well indexed, and too many have no index at all. Indexes of proper names and place-names are straightforward to prepare, but subject indexes are always difficult. The subject indexes to the C.B.A. *Archaeological Bibliography for Great Britain and Ireland* (annually) are good. It is possible to delegate a colleague to undertake the simple task of preparing an index of proper names or place-names; but it is a golden rule that an author should prepare his own subject index.

How not to do an index
Phoenicia, 1,2,3,5,6,7,
  8,10,11,12,14,16,18,19,
  20,21,22,23,25,27,28,31,
  37, etc.

How to do an index
Phoenician(s)
  art, 193–4; 217–18
  commerce and trade, ch. xii;
    middlemen, 162

Date of publication

It really is imperative for archaeological (and other) works to bear on the front or inner cover their date of publication, in order to facilitate reference at a later date. Yet within the last fourteen years at least three important archaeological publications have appeared from organizations of the highest standing, without their dates of publication: Bowen [1961]; Frere [1961]; C.B.A. [1964]. It is customary to use square brackets when the date of publication is not given but has been ascertained by other means.

Offprints

Most archaeological societies allow their authors of papers (as distinct from short notes) a certain number of offprints free. The number is usually 25, but sometimes only 12 or even 6 and occasionally none at all. As a rule the editor communicates with an author a few weeks before the final printing is done, and asks whether he desires extra offprints at his own expense. The order is then usually given direct from the author to the printer.

It is an act of courtesy to send an offprint to each person who has given material help on the project which is the subject of the report – whether by digging, preparing drawings or photographs, or writing specialist reports or in any other ways. It is also usual to send offprints to the leading specialists on the subject, who normally reciprocate.

Editors and authors should be encouraged to keep the paging of the offprint the same as that of the paper in the periodical from which it has been offprinted. The re-paging of offprints causes much confusion in subsequent referencing. If it has to be done to increase sales, the paging in the original periodical should be stated on the cover of the offprint.

The cover of each offprint should carry the title of the paper, the name of the author(s), and details of the periodical from which it is extracted, e.g., From *Proc. Prehist. Soc.* VII (1940), 203–30.

Appendix A

SOME ARCHAEOLOGICAL RECONSTRUCTIONS

PERIOD	COUNTY	SITE	ARTIST
Neolithic	ENGLAND Devon	Haldon, house site. Aileen Fox, *South West England*, 1973, 36, Fig. 5.	S. Piggott
	Wiltshire	Fussell's Lodge long barrow. P. Ashbee. *Earthen Long Barrow in Britain*, 1970, 52.	E. Fry-Stone
		West Kennet long barrow. *Antiquity*, XXXII, 1958, facing 237; also, S. Piggott, *The West Kennet Long Barrow*, 1962, facing 57.	S. Piggott
	IRELAND Cork	Rahan, gallery-grave. *J. Roy. Soc. Antiq. Ir.* LXXXVIII, 1958, 21	M. J. O'Kelly
	WALES Glamorgan-shire	St. Nicholas chambered cairn: reconstruction of funeral procession. L. V. Grinsell. *Ancient Burial-Mounds of England*, 1953, facing 47.	A. Sorrell
Neo./ Bronze Age	ENGLAND Wiltshire	Sanctuary and Woodhenge. *Archaeol. J.* XCVI (1939), 197–211.	S. Piggott
Bronze Age	ENGLAND Devon	Merivale: stone rows, etc. *Trans. Plymouth Inst.* 1830, opp. 212.	Unknown
	Sussex	Itford Hill settlement. *Proc. Prehist. Soc.*, XXIII (1957), 209.	P. Burke
	WALES Glamorgan	Pond Cairn: reconstruction of funeral ceremony. L. V. Grinsell, *Ancient Burial-Mounds of England*, 1953, facing 47. P. Ashbee, *Bronze Age Round Barrow in Britain*, 1960, facing 160.	A. Sorrell
	SCOTLAND Peebles	Cardon Glenachan Rig, homestead (LBA or IA?). *Proc. Soc. Ant. Scot.* XCII (1958–9), 24.	R. W. Feachem
Iron Age	ENGLAND Norfolk	West Harling, round house. R. R. Clarke. *East Anglia*, 1960, 95.	J. E. Turner
	Somerset	Glastonbury Lake village. A. Bulleid. *The Lake Villages of Somerset.* 3rd edn. 1938, frontispiece.	M. Forestier

PERIOD	COUNTY	SITE	ARTIST
Iron Age	Wiltshire	Colerne, Bury Wood hill-fort. *Wiltshire Archaeol. Natur. Hist. Mag.* LVIII (1963), 194.	D. Grant King
		Little Woodbury. J. & C. Hawkes, *Prehistoric Britain*, 1947, pl. XII.	Ministry of Information
	Yorkshire	Staple Howe, settlement. Brewster, T. C. M. *Excavation of Staple Howe.* 1963, Fig. 6.	S. W. Dove
	SCOTLAND Kirkcudb.	Milton Loch crannog. *Proc. Soc. Antiq. Scot.* LXXXVII (1953–4),141 & pl. XV.	S. Piggott
	Stirling	Castlehill Wood dun. *Proc. Soc. Antiq. Scot.* XC (1956–7), 45.	R. W. Feachem
		West Plean, homestead. *Proc. Soc. Antiq. Scot.* LXXXIX (1955–6), 234.	K. A. Steer
	Fife	Drumcarrow, house. *Proc. Soc. Antiq. Scot.* C (1967–8), 103.	G. S. Maxwell (?)
	WALES Caernarvon	Conway Mountain, hill-fort. *Archaeol. Camb.* CV (1956), 70.	W. E. Griffiths and A. H. A. Hogg
Roman	ENGLAND Glos.	Lydney Temple settlement. R. E. M. & T. V. Wheeler, *Excav. at Lydney Park, Glos.* 1932, facing 49.	R. E. M. Wheeler
	Hampshire	New Forest kilns. H. Sumner, *Excav. in New Forest Pottery Sites*, 1927, facing 43, 61, and 103.	H. Sumner
		Silchester, West Gate. G. C. Boon, *Roman Silchester*, 1957, 86.	T. L. Gwatkin
	Hertford- shire	St. Albans, Park Street villa. *Archaeol. J.* CII (1945), 58.	N. Davey
		Verulamium, gates. R. E. M. & T. V. Wheeler, *Verulamium*, 1936, pls. 89 and 91.	P. M. Andrews
		Verulamium, shops etc. *Univ. London Inst. Archaeol. Bull.* IV (1964), Figs. 5, 6, 7.	S. S. Frere
		Welwyn, Lockleys villa. *Antiquity* XIV, 1940, 319.	H. C. Lander
	Kent	Lullingstone villa. G. W. Meates *Lullingstone Roman Villa*, 1955, 52–3 and elsewhere.	Paul Rook

PERIOD	COUNTY	SITE	ARTIST
Roman	London	Mithraeum. R. L. S. Bruce-Mitford, ed. *Recent Archaeol. Excavations in Britain*, 1956, pls. 26, 27.	A. Sorrell
	SCOTLAND		
	Selkirk	Oakwood Fort. R.C.H.M. *Selkirkshire*, 1957, pl. 37.	R. C. H. M. Scot.
		Palewood Fort. *Proc. Soc. Antiq. Scot.* LXXXVI (1952–3), pl. XVIII.	W. G. Aitken
	WALES		
	Caernarvon	Segontium, temple of Mithras. *Archaeol. Camb.* CIX (1960), 158.	G. C. Boon
	Glamorgan	Llantwit Major villa. *Archaeol. Camb.* CII (1953), pl. I, facing 89.	A. Sorrell
Dark Ages	ENGLAND		
	Cornwall	Mawgan Porth, room of house. R. L. S. Bruce-Mitford, ed. *Recent Archaeological Excavations in Britain*, 1956, pl. 33.	A. Sorrell
	Glos.	Bourton-on-the-Water, hut. *Antiq. J.* XII (1932), facing 292.	G. C. Dunning
	Northants.	Maxey. *Medieval Archaeol.* VIII (1964), 46, Fig. 11.	P. V. Addyman
	Oxon	Dorchester-on-Thames, hut. *Archaeol. J.* CXIX (1962), 125.	S. S. Frere
	N. IRELAND		
	Down	Lismahon. *Medieval Archaeol.* III (1959), 151.	D. M. Waterman
		White Fort. *Medieval Archaeol.* V (1961), 102	D. M. Waterman
Medieval	ENGLAND		
	Surrey	Abinger Motte. *Archaeol. J.* CVII (1950), facing 29.	B. Hope-Taylor
	Warwickshire	Weoley Castle. *Medieval Archaeol.* VI–VII (1962–3), 112.	A. Oswald
	Yorkshire	Meaux, 13th century kiln. *Medieval Archaeol.* V (1961), 159.	G. K. Beaulah
Post-Medieval	ENGLAND		
	Hampshire	New Forest. Pinnick Pound. H. Sumner. *Local Papers*, 1931, 183.	H. Sumner

Note: With the single exception of Stonehenge, the reconstructions in Alan Sorrell's *Living History*, 1965, are of monuments from the Roman period onwards.

Appendix B

SOME PUBLICATIONS RECOMMENDED FOR STUDY

Excavation reports

Pitt-Rivers, A. H. L. F. *Excavations in Cranborne Chase*, 4 volumes and index volume, 1887–1905, remains a landmark in archaeological reporting. For good modern reports covering sites of several periods, see J. R. C. Hamilton, *Excavations at Jarlshof, Shetland* (Min. of Works, Archaeological Report no. 1, 1956) and L. Alcock, *Dinas Powys*, Cardiff, 1963.

For PREHISTORIC SITES, reports in the last 25 volumes of *Proc. Prehist. Soc.* cover most types of site. The Ministry of Works Archaeological Report no. 3 (W. F. Grimes, *Excavations on Defence Sites 1939/45*, I, Neolithic and Bronze Age, 1960) deals mainly with Cotswold long and round barrows; no. 4 (S. Piggott, *The West Kennet Long Barrow*, 1962) is an admirable report on a famous site. *Windmill Hill and Avebury: Excavations by Alexander Keiller 1925/39*, prepared for publication by Dr. Isobel F. Smith, is a detailed model publication from which much can be learned. *Excavations at Dorchester, Oxon*, i, 1951, by R. J. C. Atkinson and others, is an excellent report on sites on the Thames alluvium. For the Iron Age, (Sir) R. E. M. Wheeler's *Maiden Castle*, 1943, and (Sir) R. E. M. Wheeler and Miss K. M. Richardson, *Hill-Forts of Northern France*, 1957, are both classic works. Among recent reports, G. J. Wainwright, *Coygan Camp . . .*, 1967, is perhaps as good as any.

For ROMAN SITES, there are occasional papers in *J. Roman Stud.*, and since 1970 the British papers have been the subject of a separate annual volume, *Britannia*, published by the same Society. A. L. F. Rivet, *Town and Country in Roman Britain*, 2nd edn, 1964, contains bibliographies on sites of all types. Special mention must be made of C. F. C. Hawkes and M. R. Hull, *Camulodunum*, 1947; M. R. Hull, *Roman Colchester*, 1958; B. Cunliffe, *Roman Bath*, 1968; and B. Cunliffe, *Excavations at Fishbourne, 1961–1969*, I: The Site; II, The Finds, 1971. Among older reports James Curle, *Newstead, a Roman Frontier Post and its People*, is still highly esteemed. For a first class account of the excavation of a native village beyond the frontiers of the Roman Empire, see W. A. van Es, 'Wijster: a Native Village beyond the Imperial Frontier, 150–425 A.D.' (*Palaeohistoria*, XI, 1967).

For ANGLO-SAXON AND MEDIEVAL SITES, many of the best recent papers have appeared in *Medieval Archaeol*. For accounts of Iron Age hill-forts reoccupied in Post-Roman and Saxon times, see P. J. Fowler et al., *Cadbury, Congresbury, Somerset, 1968* (1970), and Leslie Alcock, *'By South Cadbury is that Camelot'*, 1972. For a good report on a Saxon cemetery see E. T. Leeds and H. de S. Shortt, *An Anglo-Saxon Cemetery at Petersfinger, near Salisbury*, 1953, obtainable from Salisbury Museum. A more recent paper is A. L. Meaney and S. C. Hawkes, *Two Anglo-Saxon Cemeteries at Winnall, Winchester, Hampshire*, 1970 (Monograph issued by the Society for Medieval Archaeology).

For POST-MEDIEVAL SITES, see the papers in *Post-Medieval Archaeol.*

For INDUSTRIAL ARCHAEOLOGY, see *J. Industrial Archaeol.* (1964 onwards) and *Trans. Newcomen Soc.*

For reports covering more than one period, see *Archaeol. J., J. Brit. Archaeol. Ass.*, and *Archaeologia.*

Non-excavational reports: field archaeology

The bibliography in the Ordnance Survey book *Field Archaeology in Great Britain* (5th edn., 1973) is comprehensive.

GENERAL STUDIES COVERING MORE THAN ONE PERIOD

Excellent accounts of regional archaeology covering all periods are given in *Archaeol. J.* from 1946 onwards, especially in the descriptions of their Summer Meetings, and also in the volumes issued by the British Association for Advancement of Science for their annual meetings since about 1950.

PREHISTORIC

The various reports on mesolithic cultures, by G. J. Wainwright, are remarkable for their clarity and concisenesss (*Proc. Prehist. Soc.* XXVI, 1960, and XXIX, 1963, and *Bull. Board Celtic Stud.* XVIII, 1959, and XIX, 1960). Another excellent paper is that by Radley and Mellars in *Proc. Prehist. Soc.* XXX, 1964, 1–24.

For distributional studies of long barrows and other monuments, see the O.S. Maps of *Neolithic Wessex* and *South Wales*, with their accompanying texts; also L. V. Grinsell, *Dorset Barrows*, 1960. The summary treatment of large numbers of round barrows is illustrated by L. V. Grinsell's *Somerset Barrows* (Supplement to *Somerset Archaeol. Natur. Hist.* CXIII and CXV) (1969, 1971), and James Dyer's 'Barrows of the Chilterns' (*Archaeol. J.* CXVI, 1959, 1–24). For stone rows, stone avenues, and stone cists, see the papers by R. Hansford Worth in *Trans. Devonshire Ass.*, almost all volumes between 1900 and 1950; the substance of these is given in his *Dartmoor*, 1953 and later reissues; there is an excellent recent paper on 'Irish Bronze Age Stone Cists', by J. Waddell (*J. Roy. Soc. Antiq. Ir.* C, 1970, 91–139).

The short leaflet guides to ancient monuments, issued by the Department of the Environment, include excellent guides to chamber tombs, stone circles, and other sites.

Iron Age and later field systems and their methods of study are fully treated by H. C. Bowen in *Ancient Fields* [1961], reissued 1970; among the best regional surveys is P. P. Rhodes, 'The Celtic Field Systems of the Berkshire Downs', *Oxoniensia*, XV, 1951, 1–28. Modern ideas and techniques in the study of hill-forts are illustrated by various authors in *Problems of the Iron Age in Southern Britain*, ed. S. S. Frere [1961], and *The Iron Age and its Hill-Forts*, ed. David Hill and Margaret Jessen, 1971.

ROMAN

It is perhaps in the nature of things that most types of Roman site get published, if at all, as the result of excavation. An exception is Roman roads, reports on which should reach the standard set by I. D. Margary in *Roman Ways in the Weald*, 1948, and *Roman Roads in Britain*, 1967. An outstanding work on Roman field antiquities generally is O. G. S. Crawford, *The Topography of Roman Scotland north of the Antonine Wall*, 1949.

DARK AGES AND MEDIEVAL

For the interpretation and reporting of linear earthworks, see B. H. St. J. O'Neil, 'Linear Earthworks: Methods of field survey', in *Antiq. J.* XXVI, 1946, 61–6; Sir Cyril

Fox, *Offa's Dyke*, 1955, and Sir Cyril and Aileen Fox, 'Wansdyke reconsidered', in *Archaeol. J.* CXV, 1958, 1–48; also J. N. L. Myres' rejoinder, 'Wansdyke and the origin of Wessex', in H. R. Trevor-Roper (ed.), *Essays in British History*, 1964. Strip-lynchets are covered by H. C. Bowen, *Ancient Fields* (1970) to which should be added P. D. Wood, 'Strip lynchets reconsidered', *Geog. J.*, 1961, 449–59; so far there appear to be no really good regional surveys. On deserted medieval villages the standard work is now M. W. Beresford and J. G. Hurst (eds), *Deserted Medieval Villages*, 1971, which contains full bibliography. Important recent studies of building stone are E. M. Jope, 'The Saxon building-stone industry in southern and midland England', *Medieval Archaeol.* VIII, 1964, 91–118, and D. M. Waterman, 'Somersetshire and other foreign building stone in medieval Ireland *c.* 1175–1400', in *Ulster J. Archaeol.* XXXIII, 1970, 63–76.

For other types of medieval site, see for example V. B. Proudfoot, 'The economy of the Irish Rath', *Medieval Archaeol.* V, 1961, 94–122; O. G. S. Crawford, *Archaeology in the Field*, 1953; M. W. Beresford and J. K. S. St. Joseph, *Medieval England: an Aerial Survey*, 1958; M. W. Beresford, *History on the Ground*, 1957; and H. E. J. Le Patourel, 'Documentary evidence and the medieval pottery industry', *Medieval Archaeol.* XII, 1968, 101–26.

INDUSTRIAL ARCHAEOLOGY

To the works mentioned in Section 1 should be added *The Industrial Archaeology of County Down*, by E. R. R. Green (Belfast, 1963); Kenneth Hudson, *Industrial Archaeology*, 1963, and R. H. Buchanan, *Industrial Archaeology in Britain*, 1972, which contains comprehensive bibliographies.

Non-excavational reports: small finds

Examples of general studies covering more than one period include V. Russell, *West Penwith Survey*, 1971, a revised series of parish check-lists covering sites and finds of all periods; and L. V. Grinsell, 'The Royce collection . . .', *Trans. Bristol Gloucestershire Archaeol. Soc.* LXXXIII (1964), 5–33, the publication of a collection formed between 1850 and 1902.

PREHISTORIC

It would take up too much space to give examples of every type of report, but a random choice of one or two reports of each period could include D. A. Roe, 'British lower and middle palaeolithic handaxe-groups', *Proc. Prehist. Soc.* XXXVI, 1968, 1–82; H. J. Case, 'Irish neolithic pottery', *Proc. Prehist. Soc.* XXVII, 1961, 174–233; W. C. Smith, 'Jade axes from the British Isles', *Proc. Prehist. Soc.* XXIX, 1963, 133–72; J. J. Taylor, 'Lunulae reconsidered', *Proc. Prehist. Soc.* XXXVI, 1970, 38–81; and K. Branigan, 'Wessex and Mycenae . . .', *Wiltshire Archaeol. Natur. Hist. Mag.* LXV, 1970, 89–107, an examination of the problem of foreign relations by a critical appraisal of the small finds. For the pre-Roman Iron Age, D. F. Allen, 'Iron currency bars in Britain', *Proc. Prehist. Soc.* XXXIII, 1967, 307–35, and J. R. Collis, 'Function and theoretical interpretations of British coinage', *World Archaeol.*, III, 1971, 71–84, provide contrasting approaches to the study of numismatic material.

ROMAN AND LATER

For the Roman period R. W. Feachem, 'Dragonesque fibulae', *Antiq. J.* XXXIII, 1951, 32–44, is a survey of a fascinating group of objects; and J. H. Williams, 'Roman building materials in the south-west', *Trans. Bristol Gloucestershire Archaeol. Soc.* XC, 1971, 95–119, shows what can be done with material of this type. For the Dark Ages, C.

Thomas, 'Imported pottery in Dark Age Western Britain', *Medieval Archaeol.* III, 1959, 89–111, and Crowfoot, E. and Hawkes, S. C., 'Early Anglo-Saxon gold braids', *Medieval Archaeol.* XI, 1967, 42–86, illustrate the treatment of very different types of material. On the border of archaeology and history are the provincial coin-mints, a recent study of one of which is L. V. Grinsell, *The Bath Mint*, 1973. For medieval and later objects, F. A. Girling, *English Merchants' Marks . . . 1400 to 1700*, 1964, was favourably reviewed. An outstanding paper based on fieldwork and the study of documents is C. C. Taylor, 'Whiteparish', *Wiltshire Archaeol. Natur. Hist. Mag.* LXII, 1967, 79–102.

Works recommended for their illustrations

The admirable books and papers by Heywood Sumner, although getting a little dated and not everyone's choice, will always repay study for their line-drawings; but it is essential to avoid mediocre imitations of his style (e.g. Grinsell, in Fowler, P. J. (1972), p. 28). Sumner's chief works are *Ancient Earthworks of Cranborne Chase*, 1913; *Ancient Earthworks of the New Forest*, 1917; and *New Forest Potteries*, 1927. The fine plans in *R.C.H.M. Dorset*, i, 1952, are in a style that incorporates the merits of Sumner's work. The drawings of stone cists on Dartmoor by R. Hansford Worth (*Dartmoor*, 1953, and nearly every volume of *Trans. Devonshire Ass.* from 1900 to 1950) are unlikely ever to be surpassed. A high standard of illustration is also achieved by the more recent Research Reports of the Society of Antiquaries, from *Maiden Castle*, 1943, onwards. The same applies to the reports from the Department of the Environment (formerly Ministry of Public Building and Works): 1, *Jarlshof*, by J. R. C. Hamilton, 1956; 2, *Clausentum*, by M. A. Cotton and P. W. Gathercole, 1958; 3, *Excavations on Defence Sites, 1939–45*, by W. F. Grimes, 1960; 4, *West Kennet Long Barrow*, by S. Piggott, 1962; 5, *The Romano-British Cemetery at Trentholme, York*, by L. P. Wenham, 1968; 6, *Excavations at Clickhimin, Shetland*, by J. R. C. Hamilton, 1968.

Superb drawings of flint implements and pottery were made by Robert Gurd (e.g. E. C. Curwen, *Archaeology of Sussex*, 1953, and M. E. Cunnington, *Woodhenge*, 1929). Fine drawings of artifacts, by C. O. Waterhouse, M.B.E., and others, are in the B.M. Guide to *Later Prehistoric Antiquities of the British Isles*, 1953 and later reprints, J. W. Brailsford, *Antiquities from Hod Hill in the Durden Collections*, 1962, and R. L. S. Bruce-Mitford, *The Sutton Hoo Ship-Burial: a Handbook*, 1972. Commendable standards of illustration have also recently been achieved by three Museum catalogues: F. K. Annable and D. D. A. Simpson, *Guide Catalogue of the Neolithic and Bronze Age Collection in Devizes Museum*, 1964; N. Langmaid and others, *Bronze Age Metalwork in Norwich Castle Museum*, 1966; and C. N. Moore and M. Rowlands, *Bronze Age Metalwork in Salisbury Museum*, 1972.

REFERENCES AND BIBLIOGRAPHY

Alexander, J. (1970). *The Directing of Archaeological Excavations*. London. Chapter iv, 69–84: The writing and publishing of the report.

Allen, D. F. [1961]. 'The origins of coinage in Britain: a reappraisal', in Frere, S. S. (editor) *Problems of the Iron Age in Southern Britain*. London. 97–308.

Anderson, M. D. (1971). *Book Indexing*. Cambridge Authors' and Printers' Guide.

Atkinson, R. J. C. (1953). *Field Archaeology*. 2nd edn. London. Part iv, 173–206: Publication of the evidence.

Barker, P. A. I(969). 'Some aspects of the excavation of timber buildings', *World Archaeol.* I(2), 220–35.

Bersu, G. (1940). 'Excavations at Little Woodbury', *Proc. Prehist. Soc.* VI, 30–111.

Biddle, M. and B. K. (1969). 'Metres, areas, and robbing', *World Archaeol.* I(2), 208–19.

Biek, L. (1963). *Archaeology and the Microscope*. London. Especially useful for specialists' reports.

Bonser, W. (1957). *An Anglo-Saxon and Celtic Bibliography (450–1087)*. Oxford.

Bonser, W. (1964). *A Romano-British Bibliography (55 B.C.–A.D. 449)*. Oxford.

Bordes, F. (1968). *The Old Stone Age*. London.

Bowen, E. G. (1972). *Britain and the Western Seaways*. London.

Bowen, H. C. (1970) [1961]. *Ancient Fields*. London.

Branigan, K. (1971). *Latimer: Belgic, Roman, Dark Age and Early Modern Farm*. Place of publication not stated.

Brodribb, A. C. and others (1968 onwards). *Excavations at Shakenoak*. Place of publication not stated.

Brodribb, C. (1970). *Drawing Archaeological Finds for Publication*. London. To be used with caution.

Brøndsted, J. (1938–40). *Danmarks Oldtid*. Copenhagen.

Brothwell, D. (1972). *Digging up Bones*. 2nd edn. London.

Burbidge, P. S. (1952). *Notes and References*. Cambridge Authors' and Printers' Guide.

Carey, G. V. (1957). *Punctuation*. Cambridge Authors' and Printers' Guide.

Carey, G. V. (1963). *Making an Index*. Cambridge Authors' and Printers' Guide.

Case, H. J. (1961). 'Irish Neolithic Pottery', *Proc. Prehist. Soc.* XXVII, 174–233.

Clark, J. G. D. (1966). 'The invasion hypothesis in British archaeology', *Antiquity*, XL, 172–89.

Clarke, D. L. (1968). *Analytical Archaeology*. London.

Clarke, D. L. (1970). *Beaker Pottery of Great Britain and Ireland*. London.

Clarke, D. L., editor (1972). *Models in Archaeology*. London.

Coles, J. M. (1963). 'Irish Bronze Age horns and their relations with Northern Europe', *Proc. Prehist. Soc.* XXIX, 326–56.

Coles, J. M. (1972). *Field Archaeology in Britain*. London.

Collins, F. H. (1973), revised by S. Beale. *Authors' and Printers' Dictionary*. 11th edn. Oxford.

Congress of Archaeological Societies (in union with the Society of Antiquaries). *Annual Bibliographies*, 1891–1900.

Conlon, V. M. (1973). *Camera Techniques in Archaeology*. London.

Cookson, M. B. (1954). *Photography for Archaeologists*. London.

Council for British Archaeology [1964]. *Romano-British Coarse Pottery: a Students' Guide*. London. Includes advice on describing and illustrating pottery.

Crawford, O. G. S. (1953a). *Archaeology in the Field*. London.

Crawford, O. G. S. (1953b). 'Publication'. *Antiquity* XXVII, 12–14.

Crutchley, B. (1964). *Preparation of Manuscripts and Correction of Proofs*. 2nd edn. Cambridge Authors' and Printers' Guide.

Cunliffe, B. (1966). 'The Somerset Levels in the Roman Period' in Thomas, C. (editor) *Rural Settlement in Roman Britain*. London. 68–73.

Cunliffe, B. W. (1969). *Roman Bath*. Society of Antiquaries Research Report no. 24. London.

Daniel, G. E. (1963). Advice to contributors. *Antiquity* XXXVII, 4–5.

Daniel, G. E. (1971). 'From Worsaae to Childe: the models of pre-history', *Proc. Prehist. Soc.* XXXVII, 140–53.

Daniel, R. (1972). 'The copy scanner', *Antiquity* XLVI, 147–8.

Davidson, G. R. (1952). *Corinth. XII. The Minor Objects*. Boston, Mass.

De Laet, S. J. (1957). *Archaeology and its Problems*. London.

Emmison, F. G. (1966). *Archives and Local History*. London.

Es, W. A. van (1967). 'Wijster: a Native Village beyond the Imperial Frontier 150–425 A.D.' *Palaeohistoria*, XI.

Evans, John (1876). 'Note on a proposed international code of symbols for use on archaeological maps', *J. Royal Anthrop. Inst.* V, 427–36.

Evens, E. D. and others (1962). 'Fourth Report . . . on the petrological identification of stone axes', *Proc. Prehist. Soc.* XXVIII, 209–66.

Ewart, K. (1952). *Copyright*. Cambridge Authors' and Printers' Guide.

Finberg, H. P. R. (1967). 'How not to write local history', in Finberg, H. P. R. and Skipp, V. H. T. (editors) *Local History: Objective and Pursuit*. Newton Abbot. 71–86.

Fleming, A. (1971). 'Territorial patterns in Bronze Age Wessex', *Proc. Prehist. Soc.* XXXVII, 138–66.

Fowler, H. W., (1965), revised by Sir E. Gowers. *Modern English Usage*. Oxford.

Fowler, P. J. (1972), editor. *Archaeology and the Landscape*. London.

Fox, C. (1932). *The Personality of Britain*. Cardiff. Later editions to 1943.

Fox, C. (1948). 'Reflections on the Archaeology of the Cambridge Region', *Cambridge Hist. J.* IX (i), 1–21.

Frere, S. S. [1961]. *Problems of the Iron Age in Southern Britain*. London.

Frere, S. (1964). 'Verulamium – then and now', *Univ. London Inst. Archaeol. Bull.* IV, 61–82.

Gomme, G. L. (1907). *Index of Archaeological Papers 1665–1890*. London.

Gowers, Sir E. (1973), revised by Sir Bruce Fraser. *The Complete Plain Words*. London. H.M.S.O.

Grimes, W. F. (1963). 'The stone circles and related monuments of Wales', in Foster, I. L. and Alcock, L. (editors) *Culture and Environment* . . . 93–152.

Grinsell, L. V. (1934). 'Bell-barrows', *Proc. Prehist. Soc. E. Anglia* VII, 203–30.

Grinsell, L. V. (1939). 'Scheme for recording the folklore of prehistoric remains', *Folklore* L, 323–32.

Grinsell, L. V. (1941). 'The Bronze Age round barrows of Wessex', *Proc. Prehist. Soc.* VII, 73–113.

Grinsell, L. V. (1957). Maps in *Victoria County History of Wiltshire*. I. Part i.

Grinsell, L. V. (1958). *The Archaeology of Wessex*. London.

Grinsell, L. V. (1962). Maps in Evens, E. D. and others (1962), q.v.

Grinsell, L. V. (1965). 'Somerset archaeology 1931–65', *Proc. Somerset Archaeol. Natur. Hist. Soc.* CIX, 47–77.

Grinsell, L. V. (1970). *The Archaeology of Exmoor*. Newton Abbot.

Hart, H. (1967). *Rules for Compositors and Readers*. 38th edn., completely revised. Oxford.

Hawkes, C. F. C. (1948). 'Britons, Romans, and Saxons in and around Salisbury and Cranborne Chase', *Archaeol. J.* CIV, 27–81.

Hoare, Sir R. C. (1812) *Ancient History of South Wiltshire*. London.

Hoare, Sir R. C. (1821). *Ancient History of North Wiltshire*. London.

Hodgkiss, A. G. (1970). *Maps for Books and Theses*. Newton Abbot.

Hodson, F. R. and others (1971). *Mathematics in the Archaeological and Historical Sciences*. London.

Hope-Taylor, B. (1966). 'Archaeological draughtsmanship. II', *Antiquity* XL, 107–113. Drawing for reduction and publication.

Hope-Taylor, B. (1967). 'Archaeological draughtsmanship. III', *Antiquity* XLI, 181–9.

Jope, E. M. (1963). 'The regional cultures of medieval Britain', in Foster, I. L. and Alcock, L. (editors) *Culture and Environment*. 327–50.

Kenrick, P. (1971). 'Aids to the drawing of finds', *Antiquity* XLV, 205–9.

Longworth, I. H. (1961). 'The primary series in the collared urn tradition', *Proc. Prehist. Soc.* XXVI, 263–306.

Lynch, F. and Burgess, C. editors (1972). *Prehistoric Man in Wales and the West: Essays in honour of Lily F. Chitty*.

Matthews, S. K. (1968). *Photography in Archaeology and Art*. London.

Mullins, E. L. C. (1968). *A Guide to the Historical and Archaeological Publications of Societies in England and Wales 1901–1933*. London.

Myres, J. N. L. (1969). *Anglo-Saxon Pottery and the Settlement of England*. Oxford.

Newcomb, R. M. (1968). 'Geographical location analysis of Iron Age settlement in West Penwith', *Cornish Archaeol.* VII, 5–13.

Newcomb, R. M. (1970). 'Spatial distribution of hill-forts in West Penwith', *Cornish Archaeol.* IX, 47–52.

Petrie, W. M. F. (1904). *Methods and Aims in Archaeology*. London.

Phillips, C. W., editor (1970). *The Fenland in Roman Times*. London.

Piggott, S. (1938). 'The Early Bronze Age in Wessex', *Proc. Prehist. Soc.* IV, 52–106.

Piggott, S. (1965). 'Archaeological draughtsmanship. I', *Antiquity* XXXIX, 165–76.

Pitt-Rivers, A. H. L. F. (1887–98). *Excavations in Cranborne Chase*. London.

Rahtz, P. A. (1964). 'Saxon and medieval palaces at Cheddar', *Medieval Archaeol.* VI–VII, 53–66.

Renfrew, Colin (1973). *Before Civilization: the Radiocarbon Revolution and Prehistoric Europe*. London.

Robinson, D. M. (1941). *Olynthus*. X. Metals and minor . . . finds. Baltimore.

Royal Society (1965). *The Preparation of Scientific Papers*. London.

Royal Commission on Historical Monuments (1960). *A Matter of Time*: an archaeological survey of the river gravels of England.

Shearing, H. A. and Christian, B. C. (1965). *Reports and How to Write Them*. London.

Simmons, H. C. (1969). *Archaeological Photography*. London.

Smith, R. H. (1970). 'An approach to the drawing of pottery and small finds for excavation reports', *World Archaeol*. II(ii), 212–28.

Sorrell, A. (1965). *Living History*. London. A book of his well-known reconstructions, with accompanying text.

Stukeley, W. (1776). *Itinerarium Curiosum*. 2nd edn. London.

Taylor, C. C. (1972). 'Maps, documents and fieldwork', in Fowler, E. (editor) *Field Survey in British Archaeology*. London. 50–9.

Terrell, J. (1971). 'Potsherd rim angles: a simple device', *Antiquity* XLV, 299–302.

Trump, D. H. (1971). 'Aids to drawing: sherd radii', *Antiquity* XLV, 150–1.

Wainwright, G. J. and Longworth, I. H. (1971). *Durrington Walls*. Society of Antiquaries Research Report no. 29. London.

Warren, P. (1972). *Myrtos: an Early Bronze Age Settlement in Crete*. London.

Webster, G. (1964). *Practical Archaeology*. 2nd edn. London. Chapter V: publication. 131–66. New edition in the press.

Wheeler, (Sir) R. E. M. (1943). *Maiden Castle*. London.

Wheeler, (Sir) R. E. M. (1954). *Archaeology from the Earth*. Oxford; later reprints in Pelican Books. Chapter XVI: publication and publicity.

Wilson, D. G. (1973). 'An open letter to archaeologists', *Antiquity*. XLVII, 264–8. This contains valuable observations on the relationship between archaeologists and scientific specialists.

INDEX